DON'T EVER START A BAND

By Phil Delta

Don't Ever Start A Band
by Phil Delta

Copyright 2021. All rights reserved

All rights reserved. No part of this book may be reproduced or transmitted in any form or by any means, electronic or mechanical, including photocopying, recording or by information storage and retrieval system, without written permission from the author, except for the inclusion of brief quotations in a review.

Cover Design: Shelby Dildine Henry
Book Design: Clyde Adams, clydeadams.com

CHAPTER 1

A BRIEF INTRODUCTION

For me, making a living in music as Phil Delta was as much, if not more of a full-time occupation than the "real" jobs I've had. Like everything in life, being the leader of my own band was a trade-off: the financial security of a button-down corporate gig for the freedom and hapless fortunes of a gypsy songman. My transition didn't happen overnight, but once music and performing really got a hold of me, there was nothing else I wanted to do.

Before that, I'd done fairly well for a kid whose mother was born to sharecroppers from Sharon, Tennessee, and whose father had to quit school in the sixth grade to go work on his uncle's farm. I was fortunate to have grown up in a small two-bedroom, single bathroom home on Rockwood Street in Memphis, Tennessee. I graduated from Treadwell High School in 1969 and began working a string of starter jobs, from flipping burgers at the local McDonald's to chopping barbecue at Leonard's Barbecue on Bellevue, now called Elvis Presley Boulevard, close to Graceland. I went to Memphis State University (now called the University of Memphis) for 2 years full-time by day, and worked nights.

I was a check-out clerk at The Market Basket, ringing-up fruits and vegetables, when I finally landed my first real money-making gig at the BF Goodrich Company. They hired me for a crew unloading tires out of boxcars, then I moved up to several other duties to be promoted to Shift Superintendent over about 50 workers in a 600,000 square-foot warehouse that housed something like 1.2 million tires. Later Goodrich officially recognized me, at age 19, as the fastest-promoted employee in the history of the company. The trade-off for working at BFG was the smell of tires, which eventually permeated your clothes, the inside of your car, your house, and even your skin. Friends and strangers alike often asked me if I had recently purchased some new rubber. I finished my remaining college requirements by attending night classes while working full-time days in the BFG office.

After I got my Bachelor's in Business Administration I was bass fishing with a work buddy out on Enid Lake in Mississippi (just south of Memphis), when he mentioned that he had gotten hired-on at the new Schlitz Brewery they had recently built in Memphis. He put in a good word for me, so I applied there and was offered a job as a can line Production Supervisor. It was actually several steps down in responsibility from what I was doing at BF Goodrich - at a salary more than double what I was making.

For two years I ran a couple of high-speed can lines that filled and packaged them into cases of four six-packs, at 3,200 cans of beer per minute each. That's around 25 cans-a-second. I was making very good money. After that I worked on a Master's degree while living for about a year in Simi Valley, California. After Schlitz had moved me to their Van Nuys brewery as an Assistant Industrial Relations Manager, I was transferred to the corporate offices as a Personnel Specialist and later promoted to a Staffing and Development Specialist. Finally, I did management recruiting and stand-up training for their corporate office in downtown Milwaukee when I was relocated there in January of '79.

After getting over the climatic shock of a full-on Great Lakes winter, I settled into my job as Personnel Management and Recruiting Specialist. The next year I began to venture out at night as a solo performer at Uno's Pizza Parlor and progressed to Holiday Inn lounges and gigs at The Ground Round restaurant on Silver Spring Road near where I was living. That's where I met the very talented Paul "Ski" Kowalski, who played in my first band. It was Paul who introduced me to Jim Ohlschmidt, a musician who became my friend and guitar mentor for some 40 years now. Jim has been invaluable to helping me organize the content of my musical story, presented here. "Ski" sadly is now departed, playing in that big band somewhere in the sky.

My experience with legitimate employment helped prepare me to be an artist and band leader who initially found all the gigs, negotiated the contracts, wrote checks and did the payroll accounting. I knew a lot about basic business principles, yet there's one big principle, the elephant in the room you try to ignore when you start a band. It's what I call, "is the gettin' worth the go?" Simply put, it means are you spending more to accomplish something than you are being rewarded for it? In strictly financial terms, the answer is almost always a resounding "no" when it comes to running a band. But there are rewards more valuable than money, like the life-long friendships with band mates and the memories of making great music, along with the misadventures like those described in this book.

When it came to cost versus pay on our traveling gigs, the whole "gettin' worth the go" concept went out the band bus window. We played everywhere from Escanaba, Michigan (when the mercury dipped to minus 70) to Myrtle Beach, South Carolina (where our roadies stole the club speakers) and even Oslo, Norway (where we were exposed to radioactive rain). When your mind is filled with dreams of stardom, and your heart feels the unconditional love and acceptance of fan loyalty - all amplified by the power of the microphone and the glare of spotlights - you never stop to ask if the gettin' is worth the go. Each gig was an adventure unlike any other. Some were like a vacation, some were a drag, but most were fulfilling to me and everyone in the band. We definitely took our chances, as they say, and if we figured what our hourly pay was, we'd have no doubt been shocked, but we'd have done it anyway. I really believe that.

This book is dedicated to many people. First and foremost to my wife Jackie and our family who have loved and supported me all along the way, and to all the musicians whose talents made Phil Delta and The River Delta Band something to be damned proud of!

I also dedicate this book to those who worked with us on our journey running sound, recording us, and providing sponsorships. Mostly, this book is humbly dedicated to the fans who consistently supported us in the venues we played. To protect the innocent, I'll refrain from calling you out too many of you, but you know who you are, and you were the magic ingredient that made this all happen. It was you, my friends, who always made the gettin' well worth the go!

Chapter 2
A WARNING

Don't ever start a band. Don't, that is, unless you are ready for the ride of a lifetime.

Among the many ways people work together, a band of musicians may be the strangest one of all. It is basically a fool's errand. Beyond who plays what instrument(s), there is practically no structure. There is very little - if any - money to be made, the hours are ridiculous, the logistics are impossible, and the odds of actually achieving any significant commercial recognition or success are a million-to-one, at best. Between dealing with band members, their wives and girlfriends (not always mutually exclusive), sound technicians, roadies, club owners, stage managers, booking agents, fans, vehicles, and the ever-present consumption of alcohol and other substances, you are lucky to keep your sanity intact. Not that there aren't rewards for those naive or delusional enough to embark on such an endeavor. Friendships among musicians usually last a lifetime, and unlike friendships that are built around more mundane things like hobbies or some shared interest, music and the experiences of performing and creating it together have a kind of depth that most non-musical people never know. When a band hits its stride and is playing together like the proverbial well-oiled machine where the music is flowing through you and language is no longer necessary, it is a priceless, exhilarating experience that few other professions can offer. Especially if it is your band.

I started my band back around 1981. I had recently moved to Milwaukee from Los Angeles, where I had begun trying my hand at singing and playing the guitar in front of people just for fun as an occasional release from the pressures of working full-time for a major American beer company. I was born and raised in Memphis, and it all started with the dreams of a little boy from "The City Of Elvis". On the quiet street of Rockwood in a modest two-bedroom home dreams came easy. I was never good at sports and was usually among the last to be picked on neighborhood ball teams. I was one of the smallest kids in the neighborhood.

One day I saw a Silvertone guitar in the good old Sears catalog, the pre-Amazon place for musical dreamers to buy string instruments since about forever (1896 to be exact). The one I looked at was the least expensive model in the Silvertone lineup - a parlor-sized box with a sunburst finish, and the strings high enough above the fingerboard to make your left hand fingertips bleed from pressing down on them. It's a wonder I stayed with it. It made my fingers hurt like hell, and like all beginners, making an F chord where all the strings could be heard clearly seemed to be an unachievable contortion of my left hand. I broke strings trying to tune them to an octave higher than they were supposed to be. Black Diamond strings were available at the local drug store, a whole set costing the full

It all began with Dennis Leake teaching me to play guitar.

month's "allowance" I received from my parents for doing chores and cutting the grass with a manual push mower. The finger pain of learning to play a cheap, badly set-up guitar didn't kill my dream. I would put on sunglasses, hold that guitar in front of the mirror, and pretend I was Elvis!

Finally, a good and patient neighbor who was about five years my senior agreed to give me guitar lessons when I was 11 years old. He owned a full sized, better-quality Silvertone guitar than mine, and the first popular tune he taught me was "Walk Don't Run" by The Ventures. After much practice I could actually play a song that was on the radio!

Next I learned Nancy Sinatra's "These Boots Are Made For Walking" which had that cool little run down on the low string. My first audience was my parents.

They were supportive, and Dad would always ask me to play "These Boots . . ." whenever we had company. Soon I kinda hated that song, because he liked it. I reckon it was my first lesson in "pleasing the crowd."

I practiced most everyday and by the time I was a teenager who could afford a better cheap guitar, I was strumming quite a few songs. This freckled faced, still short kid became a bit of a hit with the girls. I wasn't that good looking, but I was popular around the campfire on church outings and summer camps because I could play the "gee-tar" and sing songs.

I became enamored with the folk music of groups such as the Kingston Trio and Peter, Paul, and Mary. I bought all of their albums, and I still have them. After college I got a job with the Joseph Schlitz Brewing Company, and was soon transferred to the West Coast. By then I was listening to singer/songwriters like Gordon Lightfoot, Jimmy Buffet, and Jerry Jeff Walker. I had an Ovation 12-string guitar and was starting to play little "exposure" gigs for tips here and there. I even entered a talent contest at a pizza joint on a whim and came in second. The winner was a little girl who yodeled. I had forgotten a cardinal rule from the variety TV shows I had watched in the 1950s and 60s. Never follow a baton twirler, a dog act, or a kid yodeler!

When I got to Milwaukee, there was a chain of restaurants called The Ground Round that regularly hired solo acoustic performers like me. They served up complimentary buckets of stale, salted-in-the-shell peanuts that customers gobbled up (more beer!) and threw the empty shells on the floor. With three or four hours of time to fill, you might be able to repeat some songs, especially if they are requested, but otherwise you had better know 40 or 50 songs if you wanted to keep it interesting and not look like a hack. Gigs like this are where you quickly discover if being a performer was something you truly liked doing, and I did.

In 1980 the movie Urban Cowboy starring John Travolta had been a box office smash. The same guy who just a few years earlier had gotten America shaking their booty with the disco movie hit "Saturday Night Fever" had now started a whole new popular culture craze. It was out with the polyester leisure suits and flashing dance floors, and in with the fancy cowboy boots, tooled leather belts with huge silver buckles, fitted Western shirts with piping and pearl snap buttons, and lofty cowboy hats with outrageous feather bands. Urban or suburban, cowboys with pickup trucks were the new cool.

By 1981 this trend had hit Milwaukee big-time. All across the metro area bars and dance clubs with names like Pinnacle Peak, Whiskey Hollow, The Rodeo Saloon, The New Frontier, and the Country Castle were packing them in. The Tennessee whiskey distiller Jack Daniels enjoyed explosive sales as Jack-and-Coke became the cowboy cocktail of choice. Bartenders couldn't pour them fast enough. The scene was wide-open for bands that could play the "new" pop-country music and keep patrons drinking and dancing until 2 a.m. A band like that could work six or seven nights a week, every week, without even leaving town.

Between this burgeoning market and the decidedly modern sounds of the new country music, I was very much drawn to this cultural phenomenon. Being from Memphis, I always liked cowboys and most things Southern. I didn't have to pretend - I was bona-fide. And so I began what became Phil Delta and The River Delta Band.

The earliest version of the band was as ragged a bunch as you ever saw. It did include an exceptional guitar player and singer named Paul "Ski" Kowalski whom I had shared the Ground Round "stage" with, and his friend Jim Ohlschmidt, a multi-instrumentalist who played Dobro in the original lineup. Paul didn't stay too long, but Jim was on board for most of the ride, and made numerous creative contributions to the band, but I'll tell you more about him later. With my beer company connection, we were able to start playing some nice gigs right out of the chute, such as Milwaukee's Summerfest. You can't have or keep a band if you don't have gigs. Decent gigs.

Within the next few years I began attracting other experienced musicians. It wasn't long before we were playing some festivals and opening for national acts. We made a 45 rpm, a full-length LP and a live-in-the-studio cassette by the mid 1980s. We won awards. We were written up in the newspapers. I made the cover of the Milwaukee Journal/Sentinel's Let's Go weekly entertainment section. We were featured in a Channel 12 local music special alongside Leroy Airmaster and John Seiger and Semi-Twang. It was amazing how from such humble beginnings our little enterprise grew into something very respectable that we were all very proud of. And we didn't have a single yodeler!

Of course no band lasts forever. By the end of the decade much had changed. Stricter drunk-driving laws meant no more Jack-guzzling and after-hours parking lot parties. The onset of herpes and other STDs meant no more after-gig hookups in backseats or wherever. When the line-dancing craze finally came around, it brought an end to the free-wheeling days of playing the music we wanted to play. Shortly after that, it was all over.

The journey between the beginning and the end points is the real story here. The parade of incredible characters, the sequence of lucky events, the soaring highs and depressing lows, are what make this an utterly remarkable spot in time in my life. There are few things that I am more proud of. So if you think you want to start a band, or if you just love a good ride, follow me though these pages as I tell you the story of Phil Delta and The River Delta Band.

CHAPTER 3
COUNTRY OUTLAWS

From the very start of the band, it was so-called outlaw country music, mostly from Texas, that became the musical heart and soul of what we were doing. In the 1970s a "school" of outstanding songwriting emerged around the cities of Austin, Lubbock, and Luckenbach. Songwriters such Billy Joe Shaver, Townes Van Zandt, and Guy Clark got the ball rolling. When Jerry Jeff Walker arrived in Austin in the early 70s, his Viva Terlingua LP from 1973 was a landmark recording that not only established him as a great interpreter of amazing songs, but also as a talented writer himself who personified this musical movement. For one album to introduce to the world at large such amazing songs as Guy Clark's "Desperados Waiting For A Train," Gary P. Nunn's "London Homesick Blues" (the chorus of which was for years the theme for the PBS hit Austin City Limits), Michael Martin Murphy's "Backslider's Wine," Ray Wylie Hubbard's "Up Against The Wall Redneck Mothers" alongside his own good-time party anthems "Gettin' By" and "Sangria Wine" was quite an accomplishment. He certainly got my attention.

Guy Clark's first album Old No. 1 from 1975 was another outlaw masterpiece. "Rita Ballou," "L.A. Freeway," "Texas 1947," "Let Him Roll," and the aforementioned "Desperados Waiting For a Train" were - and in my opinion still are - the epitome of Texas-style songcraft. Each song is a compelling vignette with enough finely drawn characters and vivid local color to get lost in, more like three-minute novels than songs. Willie Nelson left Nashville and returned to his native Texas to follow his muse his own way. In 1976 RCA released a compilation LP called Wanted: The Outlaws featuring Willie, Waylon Jennings, Jessie Coulter, and Tompall Glazer. The album's runaway hit was Willie's duet with Waylon called "Good Hearted Woman" that became a constant request in honky tonks everywhere. If you played these places, you had better know this song. Two years later RCA released an entire LP of Willie and Waylon duets that spawned another outlaw standard called "Mammas Don't Let Your Babies Grow Up To Be Cowboys." It was a great bit of classic outlaw cowboy poetry set to a simple tune that everybody could - and would - sing along to, without prompting.

At the close of the 70s, Hank Williams, Jr. made major contributions to the outlaw country songbook and personified the music for many fans. The son of legendary honky tonk star Hank Williams, Hank Jr. had a mostly unremarkable career as a straight-ahead country singer in the late 1960s and early 70s. In 1975 he suffered a near-fatal tumble off Ajax Peak in Montana that pretty much took him out of the business for several years as he recovered. Two LPs from 1979, Family Tradition, and Whiskey Bent and Hell Bound, brought Hank Williams, Jr. completely out from under his father's immense shadow. Hank Jr. songs are anthems of a lifestyle he lived to the hilt, and his fans loved it.

Some of the greatest tunes we played in the band were by Merle Haggard. He had already made 30 LPs when he came out with Back To The Barrooms in 1980. The album includes an incredible song Merle didn't write called "Misery And Gin" that was featured in the Clint Eastwood film Bronco Billy that year. The rest of the album features some amazing songs by Hag himself, including "Think I'll Just Stay Here and Drink," "Leonard," and "Makeup and Faded Blue Jeans." A couple of his other songs, such as "It's Been A Great Afternoon" from 1978 and "Rainbow Stew" from 1981 are also Hag classics.

Another singer/songwriter I greatly admire is Hoyt Axton, who also enjoyed a career as a film actor and was a periodic guest on Johnny Carson. For many years we played "Idol Of The Band" off his 1975 Fearless LP. In '79 he put out an LP called Rusty Old Halo that includes a couple of great numbers called "Della and The Dealer" and "Wild Bull Rider." A more obscure artist who had a profound effect on me was Willis Allan Ramsey. His claim to fame was a song called "Muskrat Love" that became a big hit for the Captain and Tennille, but his self-titled one-off LP from 1972 is full of musical gems. "Goodbye Old Missoula," "Painted Ladies," and a beautiful ballad called "Angel Eyes" are particular favorites of mine.

Later on in the 1980s Steve Earl became one of my all-time favorite outlaw singer/songwriters. The three LPs he made between '86 and '88 are among my favorites, even though he's still making great music today. Pretty much every track on the albums Guitar Town, Exit 0, and Copperhead Road are a great blend of country, roots-rock, folk, and blues influences all rolled into tight, punchy songs full of attitude. I loved his song "Copperhead Road." I even bought a mandolin to play on the extended intro, and thank goodness it only involved a couple of chords. By any measure I was no mandolin player, but it helped to sound like the record. When the band came in behind me like thunder, my plunking faded into the whole sound. I never claimed to be a "Tennessee picker" but I was lucky enough to surround myself with great musicians who always kept me in the middle and never pushed me aside.

Of course, one of the main considerations when putting together a song list is tempos and what will get folks dancing. Back then, if they were dancing they were drinking, and that always made club owners less reluctant to pay you. Tunes like George Jones' "White Lightning" and Conway Twitty's "Redneckin' Love Makin' Night" were uptempo, rockin' tunes that consistently got folks on their feet, so we played them all the time. The band Alabama from Fort Payne had many mega hits in the 1980s. Their songs were, in my opinion, kinda lame compared to the great Texas writers, but they were hugely popular so we played "Big Tennessee River" and "Mountain Music" to fans who never failed to kick up their heels. Another lesson in pleasing the crowd.

There was plenty of great music for us to play, music that we could all get behind and perform with some enthusiasm and feeling. We learned to give people what they wanted without giving up what we wanted. The best thing that can happen is the music becomes an extension of who you are, onstage at least. People begin asking you to play "your" songs, instead of ones you've never heard of or have no real desire to play. That's when I knew we were doing something right.

CHAPTER 4
BOYS IN THE BAND

As I mentioned earlier, the first version of Phil Delta and The River Delta Band circa 1981 was a ragged ensemble similar to a wagon with different size wheels. Paul "Ski" Kowalski on electric guitar and harmony vocals and Jim Ohlschmidt on Dobro provided the kind of solid, competent instrumental backup that I needed behind my voice and acoustic guitar. The rhythm section was another story. A nice fellow named Hans (I forget his last name) played bass and, try as he may, he was hampered at every turn by Deeter Mantel, my first drummer. I had to rent drums for him to play because he didn't even own a set at the time! Our debut at Summerfest that June was humble, to say the least. The management wedged us into a hasty 30-minute time slot in the middle of someone else's show!

Soon after that show Hans was the first to go. I replaced him with Dennis Tickernan in time to play the State Fair in August. In September I had committed to playing several things for Schlitz, including the Memphis Music Heritage Festival and a special VIP party for the festival. By that time Paul and Deeter were both out of the band, so Jim and I played these events as a duo. The only problem with the VIP party was we needed our own sound equipment which put us in the position of having to borrow some gear locally. Luckily my brother Ken knew a friend who was a gigging musician when he wasn't working at the restaurant where they were both employed. Michael White had worked with a successful Milwaukee-area band called TRUC of America, so he had what we needed for the gig and graciously agreed to bring it over to my parents' house. Michael asked if he could sit in on guitar with us that night. He really wasn't a country picker, but he could sing, and was better versed on bass guitar than our actual bass player was. Later when Michael and I were talking he mentioned that he was considering moving back to Milwaukee before the end of the year. I told him if he did that he should look me up and I'd hire him to play bass.

After leaving Memphis we headed for Winston-Salem, N.C. where I was booked to play Carolina Street Scene. This was a huge downtown music festival Schlitz brewery put on every summer, featuring all kinds of cool local and national acts playing on stages set up in the streets. In addition to playing on my sets, Jiim managed to introduce himself to David Bromberg, an amazing picker and singer whose excellent acoustic band was among the headliners that year. Bromberg invited Jim to sit-in on Dobro with his band and a Schlitz photographer was there to snap a photo which later ran in the company newsletter. There he was, a player from my band, sitting in with an actual star. We thought that was pretty cool.

Back home in Milwaukee, it became obvious that I needed at least a four-piece band behind me if I was going to compete with the other acts in my market. Dennis just wasn't doing it for me on bass, so in November Michael moved back to Milwaukee and, boom, I had a new bass player. A good one. Shortly thereafter, two new members (who happened to be working at the same music store) were added - Mark Terek on drums, and Clinton Snell on pedal steel guitar.

Clinton had gotten his chops together in a band called Sierra, and had come up with a cool sound that blended reverb, delay, and sometimes distortion. Jim was a far better guitarist, and Clinton added great pedal steel sounds to the band, from country picking in the style of Lloyd Green, to screamin' Southern rock a la Duane Allman. Clinton preferred a kind of perfect, decked-out cowboy look - spiffy hat, classy western shirts with pearl snaps, neatly pressed jeans, and fancy boots with the pointy toes. He was the whole package.

Mark was a young, clean-cut, energetic dude who had been drumming seriously for a few years. He seemed to always be smiling, and what he may have lacked in musical finesse he more than made up for with a muscular, driving beat that got the band into gear. This was the first solid version of my band with everybody contributing their talents to make the music sound great. We went back to Memphis and Winston Salem the next year to play the Schlitz festivals again. We had great times there, and again back home playing hole-in-the-wall clubs and honky tonks around Milwaukee.

One of these places was Nick's Nicabob. When we first played there, the Nicabob was on West State Street, kitty-corner from a strip bar called Ricky's. It had a large rectangular bar inside the front door, which opened up into a room with a stage and a small dance floor on one side, and tables and chairs on the other side. Behind that was another bar. All around the walls were large, cut-out caricatures of older country music stars. Hanging below these tacky cut-out caricatures was a whole gallery of black-and-white publicity stills of more country stars. Each one was autographed, and upon close inspection there was a striking similarity in the handwriting. The stage was equipped with a few lights, and there was a metal pole smack in the middle of the stage front, right where the lead singer of the band should be.

Nick was an older, partially bald guy with those big TV-screen glasses who still wore leisure suits. His look was somewhere between a crazy professor and a used car salesman. Regular weeknight gigs were standard 9 p.m. to 1 a.m. affairs, even if there were only three people in the place at midnight. Saturday nights were the worst, when Nick booked two bands to play alternating sets until 2 a.m. You might think alternating sets with another band (often an Elvis impersonator) would give everyone a chance to fully relax between sets. Well, a twenty-minute break is usually plenty of time to get a fresh drink, do a little shake-and-howdy at the bar, and get back on the horse. Waiting an hour or more is the kiss of death. There's nothing to do other than sit in the creepy basement dressing room, or get into trouble by crossing the street to Ricky's, visiting the car for a little worry-be-gone, cozying up with some painted lady barfly, or just drinking too damned much. There's nothing quite so tedious as playing that last set, tired, drunk, with no enthusiasm for no real audience to speak of. We did it many times, and each time we'd swear it would be the last.

Around midnight on Saturdays, Nick would roll his steam table onto the dance floor. The weekly feast consisted of pink hot dogs bobbing in greasy water, flanked by buns and other fixings free to all customers so they could keep drinking. I think Nick periodically refreshed the hot dog water (and presumably the hot dogs) but I couldn't tell (not that I ever ate one). One of those Saturdays we shared the night with a familiar 1950s-style outfit called the Rockin' Robins. I guess we used their sound system that night, because by the time they loaded out of Nick's, they were so whipped they went home without taking their equipment. I later heard it sat out on the sidewalk, through the wee hours well into Sunday, when they finally retrieved it, though I'm not sure why they bothered, it being in such poor condition no one would steal it! Some years later Nick's Nicabob was destroyed by a fire, and when Nick opened a new place, all the "autographed" country star photos had miraculously survived the blaze and were back on display. My question to this day is, what the hell is a Nicabob?

Most of the audiences we played for liked to dance. The energy that dancers bring to the band makes our work more fun. Occasionally, there were hazards. At Whiskey Hollow, a little bitty place next door to the Rodeo Saloon, we played inside the front window on the floor, with only a couple of monitors between us and the four or five dancers who squeezed in between the band and the tables. This one night someone shaking a leg left a cloud of low-hanging, smouldering, ever-lasting gas. It was so bad that Michael, while playing his bass, pushed open the glass door directly behind him and leaned back to keep it open for a spell. Funny thing, we happened to be playing the Eddie Rabbit tune "Driving My Life Away" and we were all cracking up as we sang the new chorus line - "Eeeeyew, I'm driving my wife away" - while fighting back tears of laughter amid the slow-burn of someone's toxic outburst.

Chapter 5

WAY NORTH OF THE MASON-DIXON LINE

In early 1978, when I was 27, my wife at the time, Janine, and I had moved from my hometown of Memphis to Southern California. We lived in Simi Valley while I worked at the Schlitz Van Nuys Brewery for about eleven months as an Assistant IR Manager before I was promoted to the Human Relations Department at the corporate headquarters in Milwaukee. I ended up reporting to work there on January 2nd, 1979 because my flight the previous day had been cancelled due to a huge snow storm, also known as the "blizzard of '79." We had bought a home in uppity Whitefish Bay (known also as "White Folks Bay") for our relocation, and when the taxi dropped me off at the new address, I could barely see the house behind the mountain of snow the plows had pushed up off the street. I gulped, and thought, "My God . . . what have I done?"

My new neighbors and co-workers assured me the mammoth blizzard was no big deal and that epic snow falls were not uncommon. I noticed a lot of these golf-sized "antenna balls" made of styrofoam and painted day-glow colors, some with advertising logos, stuck on the tips of car radio antennae. I first thought they were decorative, but soon realized how functional they are up north. It was sometimes the only visual clue of a car coming when the snow banks otherwise blocked your view. To me it was like driving through a maze of frozen tunnels. I also learned how winter could last well into April/May in Milwaukee, and how spring quickly sprung for a few weeks before the summers got hot and sticky, followed by a nice, but brief autumn and winter's rude return after Thanksgiving. I remember thinking, "Gomer, you ain't in the South no more."

One cold winter's night back when we first started playing at The New Frontier, I hung out after the gig into the wee hours talking and pressing the flesh with folks and various hanger-on-ers. This is Wisconsin, so outside the snow is now blowing and the temperature is dropping like a bad day on the Dow-Jones. There was a good eight to ten inches of white stuff on the ground when the last "hanger-on-er" - me - walked out the door. As usual, I bid my adieu to the old man who took the cover charge, Wayne, I think, was his name. Lord, if that's right . . . then I'll be damned as to how some brain cells have survived!

I was not expecting a friggin' blizzard when I came to "work" that night, and I sure wasn't dressed for one. As usual I had on my stage boots, hat, jeans, white shirt and a long, black Johnny Cash-looking waistcoat that was thin enough so I didn't sweat too much under the lights. It was definitely not up to fending off the elements as I walked through the knee-high snow to my truck. There was one fan of the band (whose name I can't recall - so much for bragging on my hardy brain cells) who was the only other hanger-on-er in the parking lot. I remember he pulled up and asked if he could help me. I said I was fine, thanks for asking, and thanks for coming out tonight. Well, that was a mistake.

I got in, turned the key, and the starter grinding was all I heard. I pumped the gas. Tried it again. Starter grinding. I told myself, okay, kinda' pump the gas again but don't flood it, but the starter kept grinding away, and getting slower. Finally I heard the inevitable "click". So I got out and banged on the bar door to no avail until my hand hurt, then headed back to the car for refuge, such as it was. Did I mention that this was before cell phones? I began to try and figure out how not to be announced on the news tomorrow morning as "local man dies in disabled car overnight." This was before I had achieved fame so they wouldn't say "local country music star Phil Delta froze to death in his car last night." I sure didn't want to pass on without the chance of a proper homage!

I had to find the nearest pay phone, which was outside the Denny's restaurant a couple of blocks away. Dressed as I was, trudging through the snow to get there felt like an eternity. I had enough change for about three, maybe four calls. The first call, of course, was to Janine, my wife at the time. Like any sane person, she was sound asleep in our warm, cozy bed at this hour. When she answered I was so cold that my mouth wouldn't work. I said something that probably sounded like, "Ha-whoa, my wuk woo fart." Click! I fumbled for some more coins with frozen fingers that couldn't tell a dime from a nickel and dialed again. As it rang I slapped my face a little to warm up my cheeks so my mouth might function properly.

"Hello" . . . "Oft K Humy, fits me. Woo hang up!" Click.

The next call was my dying chance, so I started practicing how to talk. I was talking to myself at 3 am in the morning standing in the snow. It actually kinda' warmed my mouth up a bit. When she answered again, thank God, I said "Hummy, 'Tis Pill. Doo hang up!"

She said, "Phil?"

"Wes!"

She asked, "Are you drunk?"

I said, " Woo, Wnoo... I stuck outside."

I finally communicated my predicament, and she drove all the way out and picked me up before the snowplow got there.

That first winter of '79 I learned some new personal safety tips, like never to walk on snow with your hands in your pockets unless you don't mind losing a front tooth from slipping and planting your face smack down on the rock-hard icy paths, formerly sidewalks. I learned the finer points of fishing on a frozen lake through holes drilled with big augers, where you set little flag contraptions that spring up to signal there's a fish on while you shelter in a shanty with a heater and lots of liquor. When the flag flies up you slide your drunk ass out onto the lake ice, "boot skate" to the hole, and start pulling the line in by hand. If I was lucky and didn't fall on my butt I was rewarded with a fresh-caught Walleye or a Muskie or some other fish with teeth we don't have down south. I learned how most outdoor winter activities in Wisconsin are an excuse to drink, although that's not unique, I reckon.

I also learned that eating raw beef and onions is popular at parties and get-togethers. Yes, RAW beef. You take lean, freshly ground sirloin, mash it down on a slice of rye bread, top it with a thin slice of raw onion, sprinkle it with salt and black pepper, and you've got a Cannibal Sandwich. My first experience with this delicacy was actually when the company cafeteria Sandwich Of The Day was a "Tarzan Burger." The mighty jungle man might have wolfed-down this giant raw meat mess without hesitation, but when the cafeteria lady handed me a pound of uncooked ground beef on a bun my first words were, "Miss, ah, excuse me, Miss, someone forgot to cook my hamburger!" She instructed me to cover it with salt, black pepper, raw onions and then just "slug 'er down." Yeah, boy, definitely not in the south anymore!

CHAPTER 6

TRUCK FULL OF TURKEYS

Many of our best gigs were during the summertime, like Summerfest and the Wisconsin State Fair. The first couple years we played at the Fair were quite an experience. Part of it was driving in and out of the fairgrounds. We had to keep it to one vehicle, so we loaded everything and ourselves into the F-150 and drove - slowly - to the stage where we were performing. Those days we usually had a late afternoon-evening time slot, so the fairgrounds were definitely full of people when we arrived. Now it might not seem like such a big deal, but driving a fully loaded pickup truck through throngs of people oblivious to our vehicular presence for even a quarter-mile was nerve-wracking to say the least. Families with little kids were strolling along, enjoying a beautiful day like they're supposed to, and here we came crawling along like a truck full of turkeys, honking for them to make way so we could get to our gig. Driving out was worse because it was five or so hours later, and the driveways were even more congested with people. Of course people-watching was one of the main attractions of the Fair. Other than in a big busy airport, you never saw such a big slice of humanity. Young and old, fat and skinny, tall and short, some sober as a judge and others drunk as a skunk, they were all there at the Fair. For a few years they had these cheap airbrushed straw cowboy hats in bright blue and pink with matching fuzzy hat bands that were all the rage among women who loved whatever circusy bling everyone was wearing.

Another part of the State Fair experience was the weather. The little stage we played on the first couple of years was built of concrete, with a roof over most of the stage, facing west. The band level was about five feet off the ground. Beer was readily available in the building that faced the stage. People could meander through or hang out and dance just off the main pedestrian drag which ran behind the stage. It was a nice little set up, until the inevitable thunderstorm blew in. We'd stop playing and immediately turn off all the power on stage. These weren't gentle showers but nasty, gusty, rain-drenching squalls that rose up in the west and came racing toward Lake Michigan with a vengeance. The roof over the stage kept the backline and Mark's drums mostly dry, but everything in the front line - microphones, stands, cables, guitar effects, etc. - got soaked by all the rain blowing in sideways. The concrete stage wasn't exactly pitched to shed the puddles of water that formed during these cloudbursts. We'd try to dry things off and turn the juice back on, hoping to not get a nasty shock when we stepped back up to our mics.

It might have been that second year we played the State Fair when we also booked a three-nighter at the Gateway Tap, a friendly little bar about a block away. We'd enter the fairgrounds by early afternoon, set-up, play for four hours, pile our gear - and ourselves - back into the truck (including Mark's still-assembled drum kit) and drive out through the throngs to the west gate and over to the Gateway where we'd set-up again and play another four hours. On one trip out Mark sat and played his drums as we inched our way along. We were all young and full of it, so it was all fun and games to us. Playing together almost every day, for that many hours, made the band tight, polished, and focused.

This is not an everyday occurrence, like the regularity of going to a "real job". Why? Because it's magical. It's not sleight-of-hand, or some lip-sync trickery. It's a real phenomenon that can't be explained or predicted. At the right time and place, with the right people, it just happens. I would like to take credit, but it certainly wasn't just about me, the guy "standing in the middle." I was just one part of the whole, which was now something bigger than me. It was an extremely powerful thing.

CHAPTER 7

CAN YOU HEAR US NOW?

In the early days of Phil Delta and The River Delta Band there was no need to hire a sound system and someone to run it. The little holes-in-the-wall we played were barely big enough for the band to squeeze into, much less speaker columns, floor monitors, racks of amplifiers, and a mixing board. In those days all that was needed was a "head" - a small mixer and amplifier built into one unit - and a couple of speakers that could be raised up on poles to push our sound out into the room. Back then we amplified the vocals, my acoustic guitar, and maybe a little kick drum. Everyone else just played through their own guitar amps. It was the essence of simplicity, and it didn't require a whole lot of elbow grease to load in and out. My pickup truck with a camper top easily accommodated this small amount of gear.

As we began playing bigger clubs, more volume and more elaborate mixing of vocals and instruments became necessary. Anyone who's been in a dance club or honky tonk can tell you that people really aren't there to listen so much as they are to carry on with friends. The more folks carrying on, and the louder conversations become. As a band, you can never really exceed the volume of those conversations because as the liquor flows, people become even more boisterous. The more you turn up the volume, the louder people will talk, until nobody can really stand it and the club owner is cursing you for playing too damned loud! The answer for me was to invest in a JBL line-array system (which still fit in the truck) and to hire a competent sound technician to be listening to the room and making the band sound full and balanced at a level that doesn't overpower whatever else is going on. Those who want to listen can do so, and those who are talking don't have to shout. The acoustics of the room have a big effect, some are just noisy as hell, and they all sound different empty versus full. Adding a decent-sized PA system and soundman obviously raised our overhead, not to mention the extra time and muscle to load it all in and out every night.

One of the first soundmen I hired was Ken Aho, who did a decent job of mixing the band. He was a jovial guy with a hooting laugh who adopted the cowboy look with a hat and boots. Ken drove an older model sedan, and he kept the backseat floor literally filled with empty fast food bags. His reason for doing this was that if he had anything inside his car he didn't want anyone to steal, he could disguise it under a layer of trash and it would be safe in the smelly backseat mess.

Ken wasn't the bravest individual in situations involving the police. One night Jim, our guitarist, decided to drive his car to a remote part of the parking lot after the gig to relax a little before heading home. A squad car pulled up behind him and asked him to get out of his car. Back in those days the police weren't as militarized as they are now, and if they saw you weren't stumbling drunk or fooling around with a young girl, they didn't immediately throw the book at you. As the police were checking Jim's record for priors (which he fortunately didn't have) a second squad wheeled around to where the band was loading our equipment out. The officer driving asked us if we knew Jim, to verify that he was with us. We all just kind of stood there until Ken sheepishly volunteered "We know of him." We still laugh about that timid, non-committal comment.

There was a gig where we were booked to play in a large hall somewhere for a big dinner crowd. Once the PA system was set up, and the instruments were in place onstage, Ken began the sound check. Now, I understand the technical importance of making sure everything is coming through the system, and that each channel is adjusted or dialed-in according to the acoustics of the room. The problem was always the kick, or bass drum. Most engineers were very fond of running the kick drum loud in the mix, to give the rhythm more punch and energy, so they always tested the mic on the kick drum by itself, with the drummer hitting it - boom, boom, boom - until it sounded right. For Ken, that meant turning it up loud to determine where the peak level was. So imagine you're sitting there having a nice dinner when suddenly it sounds like a wrecking ball is bouncing off the wall of the building - BOOM, BOOM, BOOM! Folks began getting up to leave as the soundcheck went on. By the time we finished our first song, the place was pretty much empty. Needless to say we were never asked to play there again.

One of our first long road trips was for a three-night gig at K. I. Sawyer Air Force base in Michigan's Upper Peninsula. Knowing we'd be in prime fishing country, I towed my bass boat behind the F-150. For this engagement I brought along a soundman named Peter Schmidt, a friend of Michael White's who also liked to fish and had brought his own tackle. The Air Force put us up in a typical northwoods motel - fifty miles from anywhere but just a stone's throw from any number of lakes.

The day I took the bass boat out, Michael and Peter got a canoe so they could get in closer to shore and fish around the dead trees that had fallen in. Pretty soon we had whiled away the bulk of the afternoon and it was time to head back and get ready for the gig. I got the bright idea of motoring over to the canoe and throwing them a tow line, so we'd all get in to shore together. Things were going pretty well until Michael signaled from the canoe for me to accelerate, which I did. With the dock now rapidly approaching I cut the throttle and turned the boat a little, which capsized the canoe and flung Michael and Peter overboard with their belongings, including Peter's glasses. The water was all muddied now, and there was no use looking for anything that sank down in the murk near the dock. We agreed to return to the scene with a flashlight after the show, when the water might be clearer. Peter had to run the sound board that night without his glasses, although I reckon a good sound man trusts his ears more than his eyes. After the show we drove back to the lake, and put the bass boat back in the water. Then we all spent a very long time leaning on the side and peering down the narrow beam of light looking for anything shiny. Finally, Peter called out, "Hey guys, I see something!" Sure enough, off the bow there were his glasses, resting in the muck a few feet below the surface. I got the boat hook, snared the elusive spectacles, and handed them to Peter. His fishing tackle however was nowhere in sight, and suddenly he seemed more upset about losing his lures than he cared about getting his glasses back. For a second I wondered how much he really needed those glasses, when everyone let out a loud cheer for having actually retrieved something out here, on this dark lake, at almost midnight. Peter joined in the cheer, taking his glasses off and waving them in the air. That's when they slipped from his fingers and plunged back into the water. We just looked at him for a long minute.

"Dammit, I'm sorry guys," Peter said, quietly. "Hand me the flashlight."

That's when we threw him overboard.

CHAPTER 8

OUT OF WORK AND IN THE BUSINESS

A major life change was in store for me as 1983 began. I had been working full-time for the Jos. Schlitz Brewing Company, and playing with the band mostly on weekends, but now also during the week. I was hardly ever home, which put a considerable strain on my first marriage. One day at the office they told us that the company was being sold to a major competitor, Strohs. I was faced with the choice of taking a new job with the new owners in Detroit, or making a go of it as a full-time musician and bandleader. I knew at best I would only be making barely half of what I had been pulling down at Schlitz, and that I was going to have to sell the house I was mortgaged to the hilt for in Whitefish Bay. In an interview with Milwaukee Sentinel writer Avrun Lank, I said, "I had to choose between being a businessman, and doing something I love." I had already come too far with the band to stop now, and the local market for our music seemed to be really taking off. So I traded the nine-to-five life with full benefits for the nine (p.m.)-to-two (a.m.) life with no benefits playing full-time in the bars and honky tonks in and around Milwaukee. My first wife and I officially parted ways (the big D) and I got a townhouse apartment near the Northridge Shopping Center. It was sink-or-swim time, and I focused all my waking energy on becoming a success in the crazy business of music.

Around that time I wrote a song called "Suburban Cowboy" that described the scene in the bars we were playing. The chorus goes like this:

He's a Suburban Cowboy and he's never rode on the range
But he can sure get right in the honky tonks tryin' to get into something strange
Loads the jukebox with country and just a smidge of rock and roll
Because he still likes to listen to Elvis, but now he takes him with a pinch of Skoal

Okay, not exactly Texas hill country poetry, but it worked, especially with the band cranking out the punchy rhythm and hot solos. I decided to work with a studio owner and engineer named Tim Hale who ran a recording place called Horizon in Ripon, Wisconsin. It was a cozy little studio upstairs from Red's Bar, a blue-collar drinking man's hangout. The tracking for "Suburban Cowboy" was going along great until a big thunderstorm "crashed" our session. When we played back a rough mix of the finished song we discovered that a thunderclap had made it onto the drum mics. It happened at just the right time in the song so we left it in, artistic license and all.

The "flipside" of "Suburban Cowboy" was "The Auctioneer," a song that Leroy Van Dyke made popular. Lord knows how many hours I spent practicing the fast-talking auctioneer chorus, and how many more hours I spent jawing my way through it every night we gigged. I definitely had it down, as did the band, especially Clinton's country-style pedal steel playing. The two songs made a nice pair - something new and kinda rocky and a good old country nugget played by a serious band that wanted to be heard. We had the songs pressed as a 45 rpm single and started handing them out. In those days having made a record meant you had some skin in the game, that you believed enough in your talents and you had enough fan support to throw your hat in the ring alongside all other comers. It was way better than just a business card and a bunch of talk.

Once you get your record "out there" you never know who's gonna hear it. One day I got a call out of the blue from radio disc jockey Art Roberts, formerly of WLS in Chicago. I was flabbergasted! In the late 1960s and early 70s Art had a Top 40 radio show from 9 p.m. to midnight that was heard throughout much of the Midwest and Southeast. In those days all the lower powered AM radio stations signed off the air at sundown, opening the airwaves for the big clear-channel broadcasters like WLS that were on all night. I would hide my pocket transistor radio under my pillow until my parents were asleep. Then I'd switch it on, lay it under my ear with the volume turned low and listen to his show. I was only about 10 years-old and I thought it was pretty amazing to be listening to Chicago in my little bedroom far away in Tennessee. I went to sleep many nights listening to Art, who was known on the air as Chicago's "hip uncle."

Anyway, we chatted quite a while as I told him how I used to listen to him on the QT from Memphis before we got around to the reason for his call. Turns out Art had gotten a copy of our single somewhere and he wanted to use "Suburban Cowboy" for a spot in a show that he was doing called "The New Roots Of Our Country Music." Of course I immediately agreed, and he requested another copy of the record along with my bio for some background information. I sent it out promptly and it wasn't too much later that he called to say that my segment was going to air that evening. I still have a cassette recording of it that he was kind enough to mail me (and yes, I still have a cassette player hooked up to my home stereo). Art and I became friends and talked fairly often after that.

In addition to opening doors to some better gigs, our single helped me attract sponsorship from major beer companies eager to promote their brand alongside popular local and regional bands regularly doing live shows in places where beer is sold. In fact, I can't remember a time when Phil Delta and The River Delta Band didn't have an official sponsor, the last one being Harley Davidson. Since I was working full-time for Jos. Schlitz Brewing when I started the band, they were our first corporate sponsor. Typically a band sponsorships involved cash (up to $10,000 if you were a really hot act), professional photo shoots, and the production of full-color, pre-digital marketing items like large format band posters, printed schedules, and table "tents" for venues. A supply of free beer was also involved. The

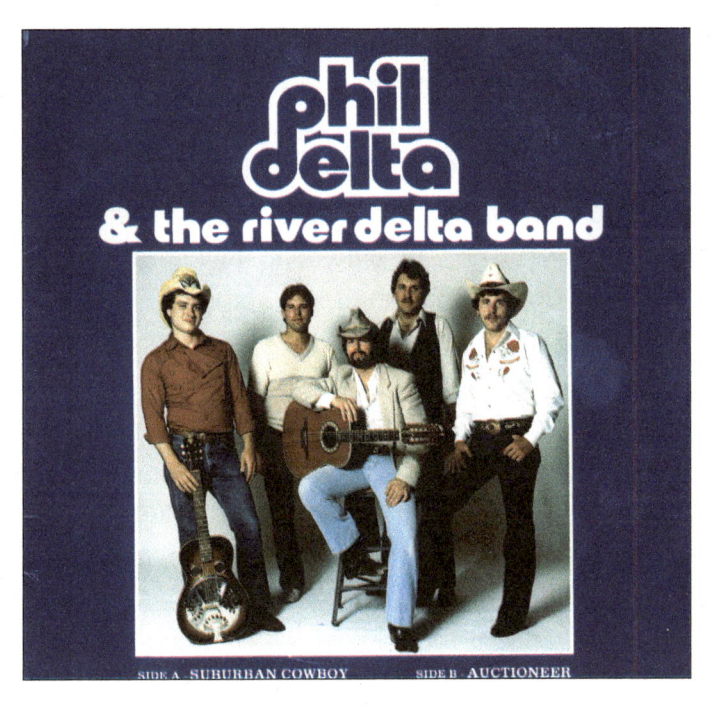

The 45rpm record jacket

early 1980s was a tumultuous time for the corporate beer industry but it allowed us to be sponsored by most of the major brands, including Pabst, Coors, and even Special Export! At least nobody in the band went thirsty.

I definitely knew how to run the business and promotional side of my band, but bandleaders must also be prepared for personnel changes. The gigs kept coming in through the summer of 1983, but my bass man, Michael, and my drummer, Mark, both left the band that fall to pursue other musical and employment opportunities. It was a significant loss considering how hard it can be replacing a rhythm section. It can be a nightmare. We tried out different drummers on gigs with Michael still on board, with erratic results. Few people in Milwaukee knew how to play country. Finally Jim and I had a promising rehearsal with two musicians who became long-time band members. Michael had recommended Daniel More (pronounced more-ray), a friend and former bandmate who was looking for work. He played bass and guitar quite well, had a great voice, and was currently doing a solo gig. The other fellow was Scott Thayer, or Scooter, who had worked with Daniel in a pop-rock band called The Answer. Neither of them had played country music, but they were good musicians who quickly learned the feel of what I was doing. They brought a new energy to the songs, giving them a certain lift, which was just what we needed. Like Clinton, Daniel was also a snappy dresser with a wardrobe including a cool silky smoking jacket, western long-sleeve snap-button shirts with metal collar points, bola ties, and matching boa skin cowboy boots and a boa belt buckle. He loved those boots, which were pricey. At the time Daniel was driving a Triumph TR7 with a manual transmission, and every time he depressed the clutch, clutch fluid squirted out on his left foot and he had to wipe it off his boot when he got to every gig.

Chapter 9

SMOKE 'EM IF YOU GOT 'EM

By January, 1984, our booking calendar was already filling up with all kinds of gigs. I still booked most of our dates myself, including Summerfest, but I was also working with a couple of local agents who got us into church festivals and other larger events that paid better than the clubs and got us in front of many more folks than we would have played to otherwise. It was "have band, will travel."

After I retired my old F-150 pickup, I bought a worn-out van from my new bass player, Daniel. I dubbed it the "blue goose." The steering wheel had about 6-inches of "play" in it, which made it especially hard to drive after you'd been drinking. Keeping that van going straight down the road was almost like a boxing match. It also had a hole in the floorboard, which came in handy one night. We had played for the closing of this particular bar, and the owner gave me an open bottle of whiskey as a farewell present. I was already too far gone to drive, so I let Jackie (whom I later married) take a turn at the wheel. She struggled to get the van out of the parking lot, and was immediately pulled over by a cop who was watching. Jackie was not drunk - she just couldn't steer this wreck of a van! While the cop and his backup had her doing Stupid Human Tricks out on the street, I poured the rest of the gifted whiskey down that hole in the floorboard, not exactly realizing that it was probably running down the gutter near Jackie's sobriety ordeal. They finally let her go, since she hadn't been drinking, or doing anything else, or maybe when they saw she was with me they felt sorry for her. They gave us a stern warning to get the van off the street asap. She drove it about two blocks (no turns) and pulled over so that I - drunk-ass me - could drive it the rest of the way home. I knew how to fight that damned beast of a steering wheel, and could drive it better blotto than a sober person could on their way to Sunday morning church!

It was early that year when I became aware of the Marlboro Talent Roundup. Phillip Morris and other tobacco giants were finding ways to work around the ban on cigarette advertising that Congress imposed in the 1970s. Flush with money that was usually earmarked for broadcast and print ads, these companies invested in other marketing schemes and Phillip Morris wisely tapped into the country music crowd. For several years they sponsored "package" tours in all major US cities featuring three big country music headliners. Someone got the idea to hold a talent contest for local country bands in each of those cities, with the winner receiving a large cash prize and a 20-minute opening spot in the big concert when it came through your town. Headlining the show coming to Milwaukee that year were Ricky Skaggs, Ronnie Milsap, and the one and only Merle Haggard. There was no way I was not going to enter us in that contest!

Obviously we weren't the only local band salivating over the stakes. The cash money would be enough to finance an entire album, and who knows what could happen if a certain someone in the business heard you and your band and decided you might be the next big thing. The dreams of musicians and fools know no bounds, so there were plenty of hopeful entries submitted on cassette tapes. The twenty best entries were chosen and those bands battled it out before a panel of judges in a couple of the local clubs. From those twenty, five finalists were chosen to compete in a final round where the winner was announced. This all happened over a couple of weeks, and when we won that final round we were the happiest bunch you ever saw! In a way it was a little unreal. We had only been together for about three years, and had just gone through a major personnel change. I guess it was the right combination of talents and personalities, along with our eclectic country sound - not to mention our little single and our busy playing schedule - that won over the judges. We definitely kicked ass on our best tunes, including the a capella intro we had worked on for "Fox On The Run." They didn't just want a really good band to win. They wanted a band people were coming to see in each city win. Sometimes there's a difference.

As soon as I had the five-thousand dollar cash prize in the bank, we embarked on recording our first and only full-length LP. Vinyl was how we listened to music then, other than the radio and television. A long-playing 33 1/3 rpm album was how you painted your masterpiece, and I wanted mine to have the best of what my band and I could do. This time I chose a studio a little closer to home. Lee Crooks at Breezeway Studio in Waukesha agreed to record and mix our project. The band was working quite a bit, so we had to book mostly daytime sessions for all the basic tracking. Jim played multiple instruments including Dobro, mandolin, and autoharp - or "auto part" as he liked to call it. He also borrowed a sweet 1960s Strat for his electric guitar work on the sessions. The songs we chose were a variety of covers we had kinda made our own, along with a new original of mine called "Spark In Your Heart." Gordon Lghtfoot's "Bend In The Water" opens side one, followed by "Spark . . ." and Guy Clark's funky "Texas Cookin.'" Next track is the aforementioned "Fox On The Run" and side one ends with my version of Willis Alan Ramsey's "Angel Eyes."

Side two opens with a Mac McAnnally tune called "Samuel Arisin'" and my version of an old gospel number called "Farther Along." They sang it at my grandmothers' funeral on an almost-in-tune upright piano. That's a sound you gotta be there to understand, and a song I had sung many, many times inside the Macon Road Church of Christ. For the album, I revamped it into an "urban cowboy" style. Yes, back then I attended that church three times a week (Sunday morning, Sunday night and Wednesday night) until I got my driver's license on the day I turned 16. Then my attendance tailed off drastically. I cannot dance very well to this day because of the Church of Christ's ban on dancing. You couldn't have sex either . . . because that could lead to dancing! Who would have thought that 15 or so years later I would be playing to packed dance floors in clubs across the Midwest that were some folks were damn-near having sex on the dance floor. The belt buckles always looked as if someone had just given them a good stern polish, but I digress . . .

Anyway, "Farther Along" seemed like a good title track for our record. The remaining songs on side two - "Painted Lady," another gem by Willis Alan Ramsey, "Suburban Cowboy," and "Auctioneer" are all from the earlier recording session we had at Horizon in Ripon with Tim Hale. Once all the "band" tracks were recorded - bass, drums, pedal steel, guitars, and vocals - the next step was overdubs, as they're called. This technique allows the band or guest musicians to add more instrumentation and vocal parts to the songs. For "Angel Eyes" I brought in Warren Weigratz, an accomplished arranger and the sax player from the band Street Life. Warren wrote a beautiful cello part for the song that was nicely played by Paul Geminder, and he also added some synthesized strings in the background. Chris Hinkle added some solid keys to the mix with piano on "Spark In Your Heart" and the church organ part for "Farther Along."

Jim got a little ambitious with the production of "Texas Cookin'." He heard a local doo-wop group called 100% Natural and thought it would be cool to have them sing backup on our version of the song. He got the four of them to come out to Breezeway on a Monday night to overdub their part. Somewhere along the way Jim got the idea it would also be cool if the singers had their own eight measures without the band playing behind them. For whatever reason, the timing was very difficult to work out and our engineer Lee spent quite a while working with the multi-track tape (no digital then) getting the band to come back in at the right time. Jim also wanted the lead singer to overdub an ad lib part over the four-part harmony they had recorded, but the singer just didn't get it. At the end of a long evening, Jim went home and filed it under "just because you can, doesn't always mean you should." It should be noted that he had already recorded and produced two of his own LPs, and since then he has played on and produced dozens of recordings (CDs) for a variety of artists, including more of his own music. Adding those black voices to "Texas Cookin'" added a really cool dimension to the project.

By the beginning of June we were ready for the final "mix-down" where all of the tracks for every song are carefully adjusted to get the sound just right before it is "mastered" and pressed into vinyl. It was also time for us to play our opening set for the Marlboro Country Music Tour's stop in MIlwaukee. Like I said, musicians and singers dream about performing in such a setting. This was the big time! We had never seen such a well-staffed, well-run situation, and we never sounded so good to ourselves onstage. The monitor system was spectacular, it was almost like listening to a record. For expediency we played through Ricky Skaggs' stage equipment, which we promptly adjusted to fit our own needs. We assumed it was okay to do that. Even if the crew had asked us not to change anything we probably would have anyway. What were they going to do... stop the show? Hell, I had already spent most of the five grand on making our record.

You cannot imagine how exhilarating and fulfilling it was to hear - and feel - the applause coming from 20,000 or so people! Hard to explain, really, what performing for an audience that size the first time does to you, but I can tell you it was an amazing feeling of worthiness, pride, honor and satisfaction - everything a local band dreams about! Then, after rounds of hugs and high fives in our dressing room we got to hang out for the rest of the evening and watch the headliners from backstage. It was quite an experience to be milling around with such amazing people. Playing with Haggard was Bakersfield legend Roy Nichols, whose signature guitar solo on "Mamma Tried" was a must-learn lick for any country guitarist worth their salt, and also Tiny Moore, the legendary electric mandolin player who had worked and recorded with Bob Wills and his Texas Playboys. The Ricky Skaggs band was full of stellar players, such as guitarist Ray Flacke, Bruce Boughton on pedal steel, and Bobby Hicks on fiddle. We were buried deep in high cotton!

The order of the headliners' appearance surprised me. It made sense for Ricky Skaggs, who was just scoring his first big hits to come on after us, but I was flabbergasted that Merle Haggard went on before Ronnie Milsap. Come on, I thought, no one trumps the Hag, at least not in my book. Luckily for me, as Skaggs was winding down I wandered backstage, and someone in the shadows caught my eye. It was Merle. So I walked over and said, "Excuse me Mr. Haggard, we just got through playing and I wanted to tell you that I am elated by being on the same bill and stage with one of my heroes."

"So ya'll won the contest?" Merle said. I replied in the affirmative and asked him if he had caught any of our performance.

"No, but they told me ya'll were good," he said.

We talked for a little while and he said that he usually sleeps in the bus until 20 minutes before he goes on. We talked a bit more, but honestly, I can't recall what it was about. I can tell you that he sounded like Merle Haggard after chugging a half a Thermos of coffee, and I probably sounded like an enamored school kid who had just met Superman! Clinton also had a little up-close chat with the Hag. Turned out they were both wearing the same boots, same style, same color.

Obviously that show was a huge success for us. To celebrate I hired a limo to drive us around the city afterward, and we even stopped at a couple of the clubs where we played, including Nick's Nicabob. A band that had lost to us in the contest was slogging through another long Saturday night when we arrived. We didn't want to rub it in so we didn't stay long, but we were sure glad to be who we were at that moment. No more Nick's for us - we hoped anyway. There was still an album to finish and release. Back then album cover art was a big deal. Unlike a single, where you slap a label on it and drop it into a white paper sleeve, here you have a two-sided, 12-inch square canvas to work with. A friend of the band, Ed O'Hare, shot some great-looking color photos of us playing on the big Milwaukee MECCA Arena stage, and we used those for the back. Jim and his friend Amy Reed set up an outdoor photo of the band standing together in a grassy field at sunset that we used on the front. A friend of Jim's, Ed Abell, created the lettering and all the other background art for a classy, professional package.

Phil accepting the band's $5,000 Marlboro Country Music check

Another friend of the band, Jeanne Muehlbauer, did all the pre-press camera work (again, no digital). Jeanne, her "sidekick" Laurie, and her roommate Amy were regular fans of the band from early on. After we started playing Hank Junior's song, "Outlaw Women",

Jeanne and Laurie declared themselves the official "Outlaw Women of Phil Delta & The River Delta Band." Jackie was the third official "Outlaw Woman" until we fell in love. We lived together a while so Jackie, her three year-old son Jonathan, and I could get to know and love each other as a new family. When we officially tied the knot on May 24th, 1987, Jonathan was our best man and I am extremely proud to call him son ever since. More about him later.

I drove to Ardent Records in Nashville to have our mixed recording "mastered," which is a fancy process that further fine-tunes your mixed recording and ultimately maximizes the fidelity in the actual grooves on the record. As he was listening to the tracks, the engineer asked me where I had gotten such great pickers way up north. I thought that was quite a compliment. As that fall came to a close, our LP was pressed, packaged, and ready to sell.

To finish this all was a big accomplishment, and we were soon rewarded with good reviews and brisk local sales. The record store where everybody in Milwaukee shopped was a big place downtown called Radio Doctors, and within two months they sold over seven hundred copies of "Farther Along." Steve Beyers of the Milwaukee Journal wrote about the album, "this is real country with its traditional gospel and bluegrass influences and songs based on real life with titles like 'Painted lady,' 'Auctioneer,' 'Texas Cookin',' and lyrics to match." It would have been nice if Steve had mentioned our original tunes, too, but that's how it goes with reviews. Another reviewer noticed and wrote, "This week, Phil Delta and The River Delta Band will unveil its first album, 'Farther Along' which will contain cover material and original songs." (Thank you Divina Infusino!) She continued that "If it holds up to the band's live performances, the record could establish the group as not only Wisconsin's best country band, but a group that can forge a spot for itself on the regional and even national level." That year we won the Wisconsin Area Music Industry (WAMI) award for Best Country Band for a second year in a row. Things were definitely coming together.

Chapter 10

GIVE US A STAGE, OR GIVE US DEATH

I can't overstate the importance of how much the band was playing then, and in places with enough room and an atmosphere to actually put on a "show." A sure way to kill a band is to book it in some crummy little joint that sucks the life out of it. One of the best rooms we played many times was The New Frontier way out on the Northwest side of town, near where I was now living. A good-sized parking lot, a nice, stand-alone building, with an efficient staff and a well-stocked bar, the New Frontier had two roomy levels and we always played upstairs. There was a good-sized stage area on the west wall, with a dance floor across the front of the stage. The rest of the room had red carpet, with two tiers of tables and chairs for good sightlines. It was a nice layout and the room itself didn't sound too bad. We had it sounding pretty good on more than one evening.

Line dancing hadn't yet taken over the "scene" and people danced however they wanted to, and there were some mighty fine two-steppers and other fancy couples out there night after night. Jack and cokes sold very well, and most of us in the band and in the audience had a certain shine on by the end of the show. As long as no one got snooty or snotty with anyone, everything was cool. We'd usually play four sets of music, so there was plenty of time for folks to dance, drink and socialize. We got to be very good at playing this gig, which for a while was a five-night engagement. All you had to do at the end of most nights was just case-up your guitar and stumble out the door.

The only time Phil Delta and the River Delta Band was upstaged was when Dancin' Dan made an appearance. None of us had ever seen the likes of Dan. He was a hillbilly break dancer. At least that's one way to describe what he did in a couple of words. He dressed in overalls, a flannel or a tee shirt (depending on the season), and athletic shoes. He wore a full beard and a variety of hillbilly slouch hats. Dan would saunter in and say howdy all around, but when he approached the dance floor, folks cut him a wide berth because this boy could move. Dan loved to show off on country hoedowns like "Auctioneer" and "Eastbound and Down" to name just a couple. He'd start dancing and doing wild, high kicks, bouncing himself off the floor, doing splits, hand springs, and generally twirling around like some kind of whiskey-fueled wildman. He could keep it going for four or five minutes! Folks loved to watch Dan and his dance-floor acrobatics. Sometimes he'd throw on a pair of those spring-loaded goggle-eye glasses to get a laugh. He belonged in Branson, but he sure livened-up the proceedings whenever he came to our gigs. I used to announce from the stage, "Stand back now 'cause you're not gonna see nothin' but elbows, assholes, and shoe soles." Dancin' Dan did not disappoint.

By far the biggest club in the MIlwaukee metro area then was Billy's Old Mill, next to the old Cold Spring

Mall. Imagine a couple of empty airplane hangars and a warehouse or two all joined together, that was the whopping size of Billy's. A long, winding bar kinda wrapped around the inside walls, and there against the back wall of this immense space was built a very large stage (by Milwaukee club standards) with an extra flashy, full-size semi-truck cab (minus the motor, fuel, and driver) with it's big wheels on a platform center-stage behind the band. The dance floor fanned-out spaciously all across the front of the stage back to where a convention hall's worth of tables and chairs were set up for drinking and dining. The restrooms were all the way up in front, by the main entrance - at the exact opposite end of the building from the stage (more about that in a minute).

We'd been playing Billy's pretty much since it opened, and did so well there that the club offered us a regular Monday night gig that we played for eight months straight. I have many memories of those nights at Billy's. Once some guy who had been peeping in the ladies room blew his cover by falling through the light fixture in the ceiling. On another night there was a couple who were so much in heat they couldn't wait to get a room and were observed by patrons having sex right there under one of the back tables. Makes me wonder how they got them to stop. A bucket of ice water? It was rumored that they both went home, changed clothes and came back to Billy's. Maybe those Church of Christ elders I spoke of earlier were right - sex does lead to dancing!

Stage with truck at Billys Old Mill

During another show Clinton had neglected to visit the men's room before the last set. He got up from his pedal steel and said to me, "Phil, I really gotta pee"!

"You were the last guy on stage," I said. "We have no more timeouts left."

Clinton considered his dilemma and said okay, but give him a minute. I knew he couldn't get all the way back to the actual restroom, when he ducked behind one of the belt buckle-high, rear tandem tires of the semi-cab behind us. There was just enough of a shadow for Clinton to hide in, and shortly he emerged smiling and relieved, with a "ready to rock" look on his face. He truly left his mark on the place that night.

Something about Monday nights at Billy's made people thirsty. Most of our fans were working folks who went into the office or wherever on many a Tuesday morning with hangovers that could stop a clock. One of the songs they liked to hear us play was Ray Wylie Hubbard's "Up Against The Wall, Redneck Mothers." The main reason why we, and every other country band out there pretty much had to play it nightly was because a whole band-and-audience call-and-response thing had been worked out (if you can call it that) and hollered out with a cult-like devotion. For those who may have forgotten, it happened on the chorus, like this:

Band - It's up against the wall Redneck Mothers! Mothers who have raised their sons so well -
Audience - SO WELL, SO WELL, SO WELL -
Band - He's thirty-four and drinking in a honky tonk. Kickin' hippies asses and raisin' hell -

Like they used to say, it wasn't much, but it was loud. At our shows it became customary for me to invite the audience up onto the stage for this bit of drunken foolishness. Sometimes at Billy's we'd have the whole audience with us up there! One night, right in the middle a rousing "SO WELL!" the stage floor suddenly dropped by what felt like six inches! We quickly admonished folks to get back down on the dance floor - as we kept playing the song - and wondered how badly we had actually broken the club's stage. It was a lucky thing nobody from OSHA was there.

Speaking of drunken foolishness, all too frequently folks in the audience at Billy's would buy shots for the band. Each time a waitress would bring out a tray with five shots of whiskey, one for each of us onstage. One night I swear folks were messing with us and had sent up at least six trays of shots in less than an hour. Man, when those shots kicked-in, I was toast! I kinda remember singing (can't remember which song) and after Clinton and Jim played their solos I was supposed to come back in with the next verse. I could see my microphone, center stage where it always was, but my feet would not move. I knew after a few little "stumble shuffles" that getting back to the mic to sing was not going to happen. Somehow I managed to signal the band to mercifully end the song. I really don't remember much else about the rest of that night, only that I couldn't let it happen again.

It was a problem because clubs like it when customers throw down twenty five or more dollars on a tray of shots, and those same customers would be miffed if their generosity to the band wasn't acknowledged and visibly consumed within a reasonable amount of time. Finally, I came up with a sharp plan. I always had a big wooden box (old Schlitz merch) that I typically put my right foot up on so I could rest my guitar on my right leg as I played and sang. Monday nights I would bring two flasks to Billy's. One flask was empty and the other filled with tea (same color as whiskey). Before showtime I'd grab some shot glasses from the bar, fill them with tea and hide them behind my wooden box. Whenever the real shots began appearing too frequently (did I mention people were crazy?), I would sometimes just acknowledge my shot and set it down behind the box. At the end of the song I would pick up one of the tea-filled shot glasses and down it after my usual toast:

"Here's to it and here's from it; and here's to it again. If you never get to it to do it to it... you'll never get to it to do it again."

You might ask what the empty flask was for. At the end of the night I would take all the leftover real shots (usually Jim Beam) and pour them into the clean flask (don't wanna taint good whiskey with tea residue) and empty it into my Bourbon decanter at home. Problem solved.

Chapter 11
LOOKING FOR AN OPENING

When Milwaukee's Summerfest began in the late 1960s, it was a pretty makeshift deal, with a temporary stage and bleachers in a field by Lake Michigan. It soon became a hugely popular music festival that, with the investment of beer company money, grew into a thriving complex on the city's lakefront during the 1970s. By the time I first played there in 1982, there were multiple live music stages, permanent seating with large restroom facilities, food and merchandise vendors, and - you guessed it - plenty of places to buy fresh beer. Each of the music stages were sponsored by a specific brewery, which originally presented a specific genre of popular music, including rock, jazz, and country. Schlitz owned the country stage for a few years, which is how I got in there with the first version of Phil Delta and The River Delta Band.

No doubt about it, getting a gig at Summerfest was a big deal for any local band, then as it is now. A performance there could either be a bust or the biggest crowd you ever played for depending on 1. The weather, 2. What the time of day you were scheduled to play, 3. What day of the festival you were booked, and 4. Who was the headline act on the stage the day you were playing. Naturally, the folks who booked the musical acts brought in the best headliners they could get, and then booked the local acts accordingly down the food chain. A noon slot was frequently a loser, whereas late afternoons/early evening slots greatly improved your chances of having a good crowd for your performance. If you had a talented, hard-working band with a record out and a beer sponsorship, and you were packing 'em into local clubs during the rest of the year, you usually ended up with a good time slot at Summerfest.

One of the advantages of being a local band on the schedule back then was you were allowed to hang out until closing. Once you had your performer badge (a sticker you put on a leg of your jeans) you were in with backstage access for the duration. This meant you seldom had to use the public restrooms (which often had long lines out the door) and you could drink free beer all the while. Each backstage area was generously supplied with half-barrels of fresh brew for all performers on that stage that day. It also meant that you might very well bump into a musical hero as you were revisiting the backstage area in the evening.

In 1983 we got to play before one of my heroes, Jerry Jeff Walker, who headlined with the Lost Gonzo Band. Both Jim and I were huge fans, so naturally we hung out backstage to watch his show close-up from the sidelines. As we stood there entranced, Jim happened to turn around and noticed that Jimmy Buffet was standing right behind us! He informed me of our esteemed company to the rear, and I introduced myself to Jimmy, another artist pretty high up on my list. Jimmy went out and joined Jerry Jeff for a couple of duets later in the set. They were old friends from back in the 1960s, when Jerry Jeff was still a solo act playing around Florida and he brought Jimmy to Key West for the first time.

Thanks to Al Guerrera and our new sponsors, the Pabst Brewing Company, we played two shows at Summerfest the next year. The first show was opening for Louise Mandrell, whose more famous sister, Barbara, had recently scored a huge country crossover hit with "If Loving You Is Wrong (I Don't Wanna Be Right)." There are three Mandrell sisters, all of whom were trained to be professional entertainers since childhood. Louise, bless her heart, did what I would call a State Fair act. Her backup band was crammed together on a tiny platform in the center, leaving the lionshare of the stage wide open for her to prance,dance, sing, and generally pander to the audience. Her cutesy, Southern girl act included costumes, patriotism, batons and flags, and a whole bunch of forgettable songs. Being a Mandrell sister, Louise had legions of female fans, who ate up her show like the cotton candy it was.

The second show was a real treat. Roy Orbison was a star's star. He was the absolute embodiment of old school rock and roll with a voice that slayed you. His catalog of popular songs is untouchable in its greatness and universal recognition. His indelible rockers are vital, and his ballads are works of orchestral majesty. Then that night, there he was, Roy Orbison, with those big dark glasses and his electric guitar, on the very stage we had just vacated. Watching this bona-fide legend play all his hits was nothing short of inspirational. Afterward as we shook hands and offered our star-struck praises, Roy was as nice as pie but he didn't hang around long, with another city to get to and a show to do the next day, and the day after, and the day after that . . .

One of the most exciting stars that we ever opened for at Summerfest was Kris Kristofferson. The runner-up to Kris was Lyle Lovett. I had caught Lyle backstage at a different show and struck up a conversation with him. He listened very carefully to everything I said. Here was a person, I thought to myself, who exemplifies the notion of "everybody's home... and all the lights are on." I mentioned to him that I was a big fan of Guy Clark, as of course Lyle also was. After we talked for five or ten minutes, I asked him to sign the brim of my hat. He wrote "Any friend of Guy, is a friend of mine! Lyle Lovett." He actually cared enough to work in something we had talked about into it, as opposed to just signing yet another autograph. I still have that hat and everytime I see it, it reminds me of how humble and impressive Lyle was to meet and speak with.

Sometimes I think we forget that big stars are people, too. An amazing example to me was Kris Kristofferson. We were well into our Summerfest set when Jim turned around and noticed that Kris was watching us from backstage. I mean, there he was, singer, songwriter, movie star, personal buddy of Willie Nelson, Kris freaking Kirstofferson, standing there watching us. He was sort of hidden to the crowd, but we could see he was actually "getting into" what he was hear-

Kris Kristofferson and Phil - Hang in there...

ing as he stood there for over 20 minutes. When Kris went on, we watched his show from the wings, and afterward Jackie and I struck up a conversation with him. He was very cordial and amiable about spending some time with us. We posed together for a picture, with his arm around my neck and mine around his. The conversation continued on because he was just very easy to talk to. Jackie and I went back to Summerfest the next night and wound up backstage where we had been the night before. A Schlitz photographer saw us and came over with what is, and always will be one of my most prized possessions. He had made a nice, eight-by-ten print of the photo he took of Kris and myself. Unbeknownst to me, he had asked Kris to autograph the matte around the photo. It said, "Hang in there Phil, there ain't many of us left! Yours, Kris." It just doesn't get much better than that in my book.

There were other stars whose shows we got to "open" for outside of Summerfest. They ran the gamut from Syliva, the one-hit-wonder whose "Nobody" song topped the charts for a while, to old Boxcar Willie, whose band dressed like locomotive engineers with those hickory-stripe caps, bandanas, and denim chore coats. Twice we opened for David Allan Coe. Being the opening act for shows like this can be tricky. First of all, you've only got about 40 minutes or so to get up there and be great. Most bands take that long to warm-up. Second, you are playing through backline equipment that the headliner uses, not your own gear, putting you further out of your comfort zone. Third, unless you bring your own sound engineer, your live mix is at the discretion of someone who has never heard your band before. Most of the time, especially at all the big shows, it worked out fine. We did our thing, didn't overplay our time, and tried not to sweat the small stuff. Opening a show was always educational, and there were many more yet to come.

CHAPTER 12

THEY CALL US THE BREEZE

Aside from hob-nobbing with the stars at Summerfest, the band and I put on quite a few miles throughout 1985. There was a ton of work for us all over the state, from Eagle River to Kenosha, from Edgerton to Janesville, from Monroe to Bailey's Harbor. If you throw a dart at a map of Wisconsin, it'll probably hit somewhere we've played. We played the Newburg Fireman's Picnic, the Saint Agnes Festival, Augtoberfest, and even a Pabst Employee Farewell Party (those brewery jobs!), to name just a few. We played the Wisconsin State Fair for the third or fourth year in a row. We even played a show at a truck stop way over in Mauston, Wis. late enough in the season that by nightfall there was heavy condensation in the air. Every time Scooter hit his crash cymbal you could see the droplets of water flying off. They had us set up in the parking lot on a flatbed truck trailer for a stage, and I don't recall that anyone was there, but that's how it was, you booked the gig and showed up on time and did your best show regardless. It was up to the organizer or parties responsible to get folks to come, especially if it's out of a band's usual territory.

Another soundman I worked with for a couple of years was Mike Burdecki, who came with his own, mostly unreliable truck and a roadie who was only slightly more reliable. Mike was a nice dude and a real rock and roll warrior with all the lines and creases in his face to verify his mileage. More than once on a gig somewhere way up north the band would arrive only to find out Mike was stranded with his truck two or three hours behind us, and was in need of a rescue.

Mike also came with a girlfriend named Rachel who was the kind of woman you would never - ever - take home to meet your parents, or even your friends. She wore too-tight miniskirts and heels, kept her dyed hair teased into a fluffy mess, and wore enough lipstick to fill a dent in your fender. Most of the time she was high and drunk enough to be a problem, but Mike somehow kept her from getting us banned from the clubs and events we were playing. Once at an outdoor gig, Rachel decided to pass out on the pavement in the shadow of the old school bus I had recently acquired for the band to travel and hang out in. She failed to notice that her head was directly behind one of the rear wheels. Thank God that when it was time to move the bus out of the parking lot, someone did a quick walk-around to make sure everything was clear. Mike was clearly embarrassed (though not surprised) by this incident, and it's unlikely that Rachel even remembered it the next day.

Mike was fearless when it came to electricity. Once we were hired by a bar that, if you can believe it, didn't have a stage or enough room inside to accommodate the band. It was decided we would play in the parking lot out back. Not only did he not have room inside, he overlooked that there was no electrical service in his parking lot. Mike didn't have a heavy-gauge extension cord long enough to reach from our "stage" area to inside the building. Where most soundmen would have thrown up their hands at this obstacle, Mike dug into a tangled menagerie of electrical stuff in his truck and produced a breaker box and some heavy gauge wire. He quickly rigged up the breaker box with the outbound end of the wire terminating into a large electrical receptacle box for his sound system and our guitar amps. Fine, but where would he feed the box from? Mike saw that there was a telephone pole carrying a live electrical line in the back of the parking lot. He rigged up two big alligator clamps for the positive and negative feeds to the breaker box, then used a metal extension ladder to get up the telephone pole and attached the positive alligator clamp to the raw power line - carrying extremely high voltage - and clamped the negative clamp onto a neutral line somewhere.

The utility company puts those lines way up at the very top of the pole and separates them far apart for a reason. If, God forbid, some crazy person would ever touch the positive and a ground line at the same time it would mean certain electrocution, not to mention a loss of power to the surrounding area. But that didn't worry Mike. He knew what he was doing. I remember his breaker box just hanging there, about three quarters of the way down that pole, feeding us the power for our gig to go on. The really scary part was after a four-plus hour show, during which Mike indulged in his usual consumption, he had to climb back up and remove the alligator clamps. Mike enlisted our drummer,

Scooter, to spot him as his safety man. "If I start sparking, kick the ladder out from under me," he told him! Once again, it was a good thing no one from OSHA was around. We'd have been fined up the wazoo, along with the bar owner. Just another gig for Mike, though.

After our busy summer of criss-crossing the state, in October we loaded up the old band bus and took off on our biggest road adventure to date. We had taken a four-night engagement playing in the NCO Club at the Myrtle Beach Air Force Base. I booked this through an agency so there were a few perks. We had rooms at a beachfront motel, and the facility had its own PA speakers, which saved us from having to lug ours. Otherwise it was a 24-hour drive each way, and so we did our best to make ourselves at home in this former school bus missing most of the original seats and now furnished with a couch and some other old furniture. We walled-off a section in the back with some plywood where we stowed our equipment which we loaded from the back door of the bus. Dan helped to coordinate two roadies in Myrtle Beach for us. They were old friends of his, or something.

This old school bus we traveled in, like most good old school buses, ran pretty good but was worn-out from decades of picking up and dropping off school kids. Especially the steering wheel. It was as bad as that van I had bought from Daniel when the F-150 was done. Once again, nobody but me could drive this damn bus without having a wreck or putting us in

Band on bus to Myrtle Beach gig

the ditch. Anyone else who tried was more than willing to let me do it. We had just gotten a new sponsorship with Coors, which had gone non-union and were not looked upon kindly for it. So between cars angrily passing this lumbering old bus weaving all over the road (at least when Jim tried driving) and then seeing the giant Coors logo on the back door . . . well, let's just say it wasn't pretty.

To insure we'd arrive in mostly one piece, I took the wheel for most of the all night drive. Clinton had appropriated some "uppers" from his aunt's medicine bottle (or somewhere) so I loaded up on those and kept on truckin'. Scooter was my co-pilot, always sitting to my right and helping me navigate. He finally needed a little sleep, and after he nodded off he was jolted awake when I started hollering, "Beavers! Look at the hundreds of beavers on the side of the road!"

He woke up and saw the "beavers." A recent rain had washed out some newly sodded area of the roadside and hundreds of beaver-looking clumps of sod had washed down to the edge of the pavement. A few more silent miles down the road and I said, to no one in particular, "I still think they were beavers." Fatigue will do strange things to a person's mind, or what's left of it. We finally made it to Myrtle Beach after sunrise and found our motel. Those beds felt good.

The two roadies Daniel had lined up to help us were more country than cornflakes. One prefaced or ended everything he uttered with the phrase "you know". But when he drawled it, it sounded more like "Yeeeew now." Being in our motel on the oceanfront was nice, with a few spectacular sunrises. The gig was no big deal, and we played our show for a bunch of nice military folks who didn't know us from Adam. They seemed to like us, as most people did. When the last night was over the roadies basically decided they weren't making enough money and they made up for their loss by stealing the PA speakers that belonged to the base by putting them in the back of our bus last, in front of our gear, and unloaded them when we dropped them off. I'm pretty sure the law takes a dim view of stealing military-owned equipment, but once the "missing" speakers were discovered, I made sure they were returned asap (Daniel got on their case, too, since they were his "friends") with a full apology to the military brass.

The morning after that last night of playing at the base (I am absolutely sure that we were all still legally drunk) the "Triple Crown" combination of lingering inebriation, an empty stomach (I was starving) and a case of exasperation made a joke that Mr. "Yeeew now" told us seem a hundred times more hilarious than it actually was. It went like this:

"A priest was walking down the sidewalk when he met a little kid with a glass bottle of clear liquid sitting on a curb. The priest stopped and asked the boy, 'What have you got in the bottle my son?' The little boy, (in a familiar drawl) said, 'Father, this here is the most powerful liquid in the world, and I just proved it before you walked up.' The priest replied, 'Now son, that can't be true! Holy water is the most powerful liquid in the world. Why, if you rub some holy water on a pregnant woman's belly, she will pass her baby.' The boy looked at the priest and said, 'Well, I don't know about that, Father, but this here's turpentine. If you rub some of this on a cat's ass, it'll pass a motorcycle.'" It was one of those jokes, told just the right way, at the right time, that had us laughing until we damn near cried. We packed up and left Myrtle Beach later that day with a little money in our pockets, eager to get back home but satisfied that we had made our first big road trip, warts and all. I drove most of the way back, of course, wrestling with that damned steering wheel like the worn-out bus pro I was. By the time we got back to Milwaukee we were all in agreement that we had had enough of that, for now anyway.

Our next road gig was a little closer to home in Land O Lakes, north of Eagle River on the state line between Wisconsin and the Upper Peninsula of Michigan where we were hired to play a wedding. To most bands, wedding gigs are great. They typically pay quite a bit more than a club date or even some festivals because the parents of the bride are basically on an obligatory spending spree. Tradition still holds that the bride's folks pick up the tab for the reception, which is a much bigger cash outlay than for the rehearsal dinner the night before the wedding paid for by the groom's family. I've pondered this disparity in costs and have rationalized it as a possible carryback to the old days when brides' families offered a "dowry" for their daughters to get them married off, the less attractive the bride the larger the dowry. Anyway, if one or both of the betrothed were fans of our band, they were often motivated to pay more. Sometimes a lot more.

There is a downside to wedding gigs that most times made these blissful martial gatherings a nightmare for us because we were not a wedding band. It typically played out like this - the bride and groom and usually most of the wedding party were our fans, or at least knew of us and the music we played. They two-stepped and waltzed the night away, having a great time. Then there were the rest of the folks, who had never heard of us, some of whom didn't necessarily like country music, or even hated it. On top of that we didn't play too many Top 40 country songs that were heard on the radio. It was not uncommon during a wedding gig of ours to hear a drunken uncle shout out "Play Proud Mary," or "Stairway To Heaven, dude" or some other request that was obviously way out of our genre. I would usually apologize and say, "Sorry, we don't know that one, but maybe you'll like this one" and roll into a preferably uptempo song that would get everybody dancing which quickly overruled the request. Some wedding folks took it well, but some didn't. Most of them never remembered it by the next morning anyway. Despite some big bucks to be made, we generally avoided playing for weddings.

The wedding in Land O Lakes was an extreme and welcome exception to the norm. It was definitely the most lavish, fun and memorable wedding we ever played. For starters it involved two consecutive nights of playing. The groom and his bride loved our band. He was a dentist who went by the nickname "Painless." I can tell you, those two gigs were definitely painless for us. The first reception was in Milwaukee at a real top-shelf, swanky venue, and the second reception was way up north. It was a bit of a "hoof" to get there, but it was well worth it. It took place in a very cool old rustic facility called Barefoot Charlies, a huge log-built structure that was perfect for a party like this. The band was put up in a nice local motel. We found out a little later that Painless handled all the town's fireworks. He had a bunker full of Class A ordnance. The band and I were kicking back outside the motel after our show that night when at the stroke of midnight we heard an earth-shaking KA-BOOM!!!. We all just looked at each other and exclaimed, almost in unison, "Painless!" Many in the hard-dancing, well-served crowd in attendance had driven up from Milwaukee for this cool "twofer" reception, and we all gathered outside for an amazing fireworks display complete with some of those cool "light up, whirl, whistle and explode" sign-mounted fiery displays. There was even a giant, customized one that showed two pairs of feet - one on the bottom with the toes spread outward and another pair of feet on top with the toes pointing inward, with the names of the bride and groom lighting up accordingly with their appropriate celebratory ending position.

All that would have been plenty, but after a hearty breakfast the next morning Painless invited us down to his dental office for a "free checkup". It was certainly not your usual dental office visit. After taking a quick look at our respective choppers he sat us down in another chair and put a gas mask on us, slowly turning up the nitrous oxide to a level just short of what felt like brain damage. WOW!!! Each of us hallucinated, tried to talk and kinda freaked out in different ways. Daniel gave us the most memorable response. When he hit the max gas level he ripped off the mask, jumped out of the chair, and after a few dazed seconds blurted out the best drug-induced epiphany I've ever heard. "Everything is soooo important . . . Yet nothing matters!"

CHAPTER 13

THE GREAT NORTHERN CHALLENGE

To me, the Great Northern Challenge meant getting to the gig in the middle of winter without a breakdown, playing the gig, and getting back home without freezing your ass off or otherwise perishing. In terms of my previously mentioned "Is The Gettin' Worth The Go" calculation, the gigs I am about to tell you of were NOT worth the go in any real way, shape, or form. They were arranged for us one winter by a certain booking agent and, like Rod Serling, I will present them for your reading pleasure, preferably from the warmth of your fireside. We begin with one of the less life-threatening situations before finishing with the one that almost killed me.

For a while we played in Green Bay (known as "Title Town" to Packers fans, like me) at a club that booked us by the week and put us up at the lovely Title Town Motel. Most winter gigs went pretty well, up north, in the land of Jagermeister shots and traditional "Boilermakers". For those less experienced drinkers, Boilermakers are a unique drink where the barkeep brings you a glass of beer and a shot of whiskey. You drop the shot, glass and all, into the mug of beer and slug 'er on down (being careful not to break a tooth when the shot glass slides down.) During our show I would throw in a few team cheers - "Go Pack!" and so on, which was always good for at least one round of shots for the band. Green Bay is pretty cold in the winter, but by the time we started working regularly up there I was getting used to the winter weather. I was about as "broke-in" on cold temps as a Memphis boy could get. Turns out Green Bay was nothing compared with the winter wonderland that was coming.

Escanaba, Michigan is pretty far north, so this gig was challenging in terms of time and distance. It was a week-long gig, Monday through Saturday night - in a bowling alley! Well, as fate had it we were running late on our arrival time. It was us five musicians - some who rode with me in the bus and others who drove themselves - and the sound crew, who drove up in their mechanically challenged box truck. I knew before we left that we'd be late, probably significantly late, so being a responsible band leader I called the bar manager and let him know. He wasn't too happy but said to hurry up as best we could because people were already there to hear the band. I estimated we'd be about 30 minutes late plus setup time, which was not good.

As we crossed the state line a sign informed us that Michigan was in the Eastern Time Zone. Crap!!! Now we were actually an hour and thirty minutes late, plus setup . . . There's nothing quite so (un)professional as having an audience (or what was left of it by the time we arrived) watch an award-winning band from the big town of Milwaukee suffer through a hurried setup and sound check. We finally started playing about two hours late. The layout wasn't bad for a bowling joint, with a stage between the bar and the alleys. Bowlers in Northern Wisconsin were pretty serious drinkers and so we prayed for a good time to be had by all. Man, were we wrong! We ended our first up-tempo tune with a big finish and . . . you could hear a pin drop, literally - bowling pins. Turns out this was an establishment that routinely booked 50's & 60's cover bands, and rock acts. We drank more than our share of Boilermakers that night and cursed the agent that sent us to this place. We had to try and fit in somehow, and later on we managed to stir up a few country/country rock fans. It was like a weird country song, "Headaches Out of Boilermakers," or something.

The next gig in the Great Northern Challenge was at a bar whose name I can't recall but I do remember that it was smack dab in the middle of freaking nowhere. We drove down a long, slippery, winding road, dodging deer and downed tree limbs while trying to keep the bus wheels in the snow ruts, when suddenly out of nowhere a large wooden building that looked like a shack appeared. Lights were on inside, so this was the place. It was snowing like crazy that night, with almost a foot already on the ground when we arrived. Inside the bar were four or five patrons holding down barstools. There was a small "stage" raised up off the floor over in the corner, which we considered a good sign. The foremost question on our mind was who in the hell is gonna come way out here in a snowstorm to hear a band? We were there, so we set up and did a sound check, then began to drink and mingle with the regulars. They were real friendly folks and I began to think that if nothing else we could at least have a good time at the bar. When our nine o'clock came around and not another soul had walked through the door, so it was tempting to just keep drinking and hope for more folks to show up, but the last thing I wanted to cultivate up north was a reputation for starting late so we played our first set. The few folks there politely applauded a lot so we sat down with them during our break, thinking "the show must go on." All of a sudden we heard something in the distance that sounded like a herd of lawn mowers. It was snowmobiles - LOTS of snowmobiles! Looking out the window, we could see a long string of bobbing headlights heading towards us. Twenty five or so snowmobiles, many with drivers and riders, pulled up, parked and stormed into the club. Our newly arrived audience were out bar hopping and were already primed. We kicked off the second set as more snowmobilers arrived. Before we knew it, there was one helluva crowd! We had a great night and there was a nearby motel where we enjoyed a good night's sleep after all that merriment.

The final leg of the Great Northern Challenge took place one November, which is still technically fall, right?. The weather can be brutally unpredictable around upper Lake Michigan and eastern Lake Superior, especially in November. Earlier in my musical career playing as a single act I must have sang Gordon Lightfoot's "The Wreck Of The Edmund Fitzgerald" hundreds of times, but this Southern boy didn't quite get his head around the danger implied by the lyrics:

Lake Huron rolls, Superior sings
In the rooms of her ice-water mansion
Old Michigan steams like a young man's dreams
The islands and and bays are for sportsmen
And farther below Lake Ontario
Takes in what Lake Erie can send her
And the iron boats go as the mariners all know
With the gales of November remembered

We had a gig booked in Eagle River, which sounded harmless enough but turned out to be the coldest experience of my life. I'm not sure what prompted it, but this gig became a big "bring your friend or a partner" thing. Jackie and I were the only ones who rode up in the bus. Everybody else in the band drove themselves along with their partner or girlfriend, so we brought a small audience with us, and we all got separate rooms in a local fleabag hotel. It was a weekend gig so we started Friday night, with the mercury dipping just a few degrees below zero. By the end of Saturday night a massive Canadian air mass moved in and the temperature plummeted to 35 or 40 below, with a minus-70 windchill. I remember stepping outside and watching my breath instantly freeze on my moustache. The heaters in our cheap rooms barely kept it in the 40's and some of the sewer lines froze, leaving Jackie and I without a working toilet. Stepping outside to take a leak was not advisable. It froze before it hit the ground.

The next morning we had to put three of our 500w stage lights under the oil pan to get the bus cranked and running. I let it "warm up" for a half hour or so and it was still freezing inside. It had a small heater in front, blowing on the driver's feet, which did little to nothing inside the frosty cab. We realized we were in for a long, cold ride home. There was one bench seat to the right and behind the driver's seat where Jackie sat. We commandeered a couple of hotel blankets and hung them as best we could behind that bench seat to seal off the twenty or so feet of open space behind us. Then we layered up with as many clothes as possible and began our frigid trek back to Milwaukee.

    The straight line winds were blowing in like a hurricane from the west, and the passenger door which didn't seal all that well let in a lot of icy wind as we drove along. We crammed rags, towels and anything else we could find to try and seal the gaps, but snow began accumulating inside the door. It did not melt. The slick, snow-strewn roads made for a harrowing ride home that could have been extremely dangerous for us had the bus conked out. It got us all the way home and we didn't lose any fingers, toes, ear lobes or other appendages. I remember hearing harp music as we walked into our lovely, warm house.

Chapter 14
JUST A LITTLE OUT OF HAND

Back in MIlwaukee we kept busy playing the clubs and performing at holiday parties for employees of Quad Graphics, and a big Oldsmobile car dealership. The absolutely best paying night of the year for club bands like us was New Year's Eve, and that year we scored a real humdinger of a gig at one of the nearby Holiday Inn hotels. I got us a nice, fat payment to play from 9 to 2, and also got the hotel manager to comp each band and crew member a hotel room of their own to crash in after the show. This included two rooms for our soundman, Jeff Shaffer, and his roadie, Keith. Jeff was a tall, kinda geeky guy with a punk haircut and was one of the first people I knew to own a cellular telephone, which back then was a bulky affair he carried in a shoulder bag. Keith was a little wet behind the ears, but he was always smiling and was a pleasure to be around.

Overall, the night was a huge success. The cover charge was pricey, but our fans ponied up for the biggest non-festival Phil Deta and The River Delta Band show of the year. Apparently the demand for tickets was such that the hotel manager got greedy and didn't stop selling tickets after the main room was sold out. Without telling us, or our ticket-buying fans, he decided to handle the overflow by adding another room adjacent to the main room where we were playing. Of course you couldn't see the stage from that second room, so he jerry-rigged a camera and a remote screen and speakers in the second room which conveniently was separated from the main room by the bar. His plan worked out okay, although I'm sure the attendees arriving to find that their tables were not in the main room were more than a bit disappointed. Most of them just crowded in the main room anyway and stood to watch the show.

Things were going well, the DJ played music for the early arrivers and our show kicked off with a bang! It was one of those nights when we were all in the groove and the first set rocked and was met with a great, enthusiastic response and many trays of shots for the band. We played a good long set and wrapped up just in time to relieve ourselves and make a quick trip to our rooms for a breather. As I headed to my room someone said the hotel manager was looking for me. I found him and he said straight-out, "We have a problem."

Keith was so proud of having his own hotel room that he invited a ton of his young friends who weren't really big fans of the band. While we were out there working, they had spent the whole first set drinking and partying. In this case when I say partying, I mean seriously drunken, disgusting and destructive behavior. When the manager opened the door to Keith's room, I couldn't believe my eyes! I've seen some trashed hotel rooms in my life, but this one would've made Joe Walsh blush. Walking into the room I could feel the carpet squish with puke, spilled drinks, and worse under my boots. The curtains were torn from the windows, brackets and all. The little wooden ledge for the phone to set on was broken off and laying on the floor, and mirrors were torn off the walls. The bed spreads were soaked with the same vile, putrid liquids as the carpeting. I thought I had seen it all, until the manager opened the bathroom door. There, laying in the bathtub, totally naked, with the clear shower liner wrapped around him was some guy who had apparently twirled in circles while projectile vomiting over every inch of the shower. For a minute I had to marvel at the kid's agility!

Unfortunately I will never forget that sight, nor the night. It goes without saying that Keith did not get the New Year's Eve bonus that I had planned for him. It fell well short of what it cost me to have the room fixed. He felt absolutely terrible about it later, knowing he had messed-up big-time. It was almost a fitting end to one helluva year. The strength of our sound and our presence as a band, and the support of our many fans could overcome and correct for just about any wrench thrown into the works by roadies or anyone else. It was time again to look forward and keep my eyes on the prize.

Chapter 15

THE 4,000 MILE GIG

Booking agents are notorious for lame dates and bad routing, but I was lucky to be working with several good ones. They included John Mangold (good name for a business guy) and his organization Talent Associates, a local agency in our primary market that got us some great regional work. I was also associated with The Robert Kenny Agency and ACA. This took some of the load off of me to book and coordinate every single gig. I kept on booking all our local club dates, along with some of the festivals and special events I already had good relations with. Professional representation from these agencies potentially bumped us up in line for bigger and better opportunities, and helped get us work we might have missed on our own. With our debut album, we were definitely a viable act.

When I was approached by ACA Music & Entertainment Corporation, they had two offices, one in Punta Gorda, Florida and the other in Milwaukee. ACA, in conjunction with the Joelle Lewis Agency, soon offered us a two-month gig in Oslo, Norway. Now that was cool and exciting in a number of ways, but there was also a whole lot to consider in accepting this offer. A big thing in its favor was being a club gig, where we would play in one place until the engagement was over. No moving and hauling equipment, no trying to figure out where the next gig was, no staying in all kinds of strange places. Just go to work every night and come back to your (little) sleeping room. In addition to our wages, the gig included airfare, lodging and two meals per diem. The club was smack downtown in a historic 18th-century dining hall and beer joint called the Gamle Christiania, which featured American country bands six nights a week. There was plenty of room for dancing, and we definitely knew how to play for that! The big gamble was whether the folks who hung out there weekly would actually like us. It could be an awfully long two months if they didn't. I had faith that the booking agents knew what they were doing.

Leaving home for an extended time was another big consideration. Luckily, Jackie was very supportive. For her it would be a sacrifice, and a strain on her already busy schedule. I was normally home during the day, so I took care of our two dogs, Asphen and Maliboo, while she was working full-time. Now she'd have to figure out a way to run home mid-day and tend to the herd's feeding and potty needs. Mainly, her safe "security blanket" (me) would be gone. Her life would be lonely and more hectic while I was off galavanting in a far-off land doing what I love. Hardly a fair deal, but she saw how much we all (the band) wanted to do this. Unconditional love can overcome a lot of things in life, and after more than thirty-five years together now, I know it's true! How I ever became so lucky in the first place may be the subject of my next book.

Then there were the four other band members to get on board otherwise it was a no-go. Each had his own situation to deal with. For a musician living with

Band on the KLM flight to Oslo, Norway

a girlfriend who is just a break-up away from becoming homeless, being gone for two months can be a scary prospect. You might come back to find another man drinking your liquor and petting your dog, as they say. Seriously though, rent and bills needed paying meanwhile, which meant opening a Norwegian bank account to convert our kroner into US dollars and send checks back home. Those living in the city with parking regulations had to find a safe, non-ticketable place to keep their vehicle. The list goes on . . . The truth was we were getting a little burned-out in the local clubs, so disappearing for a while didn't sound like such a bad idea. It might boost demand for us when we came back. Besides, who knows what really cool things might happen, say the dreams of musicians and fools.

I had never been outside the country, much less flown across the Atlantic Ocean. Daniel was the only band member who had been overseas. The rest of us got our passports expedited through the consulate in Chicago. The Gamle Christiania provided backline equipment, but we brought our own guitars, I brought my microphone, and Clinton brought his pedal steel and a cool vintage lap steel he played on some songs. On the big day of our departure, we bid anxious good-byes to our significant others who drove us to O'Hare airport. We handed-off our instruments to the baggage crew with a prayer that they would arrive at our destination in one piece. Like all international flights it was a big plane with lots of people, and we were seated next to each other in the same row. As we chit-chatted about the flight plan, a couple of band members proposed leaving the Amsterdam airport to visit a hash bar during our layover there, but I rode herd on that fool notion. Not that they were serious, exactly (at least I don't think they were), but it sure gave me a feeling of not being in Wisconsin anymore. The impact of what we were actually doing finally hit me, we're flying damn-near halfway around the world to play an extended gig in a country we've never set foot in and don't know the language. What could possibly go wrong?

Chapter 16

OFF AND RUNNING

We arrived in Oslo the day our gig began. Jet-lagged and hungover, we took in our new surroundings - city streets lined with very old buildings and sidewalks crowded with people. It was March 1st, with a fair amount of snow on the ground but not quite as cold as back home. A representative from the booking agency found and guided us east of downtown to a tall, four-story fortress-looking place at Urtegata 31. With fancy arched brickwork like raised eyebrows over the windows, and a vaulted roof crowned with a steeple and a crucifix, we were told this imposing architectural antique had been a convent. It now housed the acts who played the booking agency's various accounts downtown. Inside, the building was mostly clean, and as spartan as a nunnery can be. You could say that as musicians, we too had taken a vow of poverty, but there was nothing particularly pious about our time at Urtegata 31. Each of our rooms had a bed, a sink, and a mini-fridge. Bathrooms with showers were at each end of the hall on each floor. Two full-time housekeepers kept the place from turning into a pigsty, and a "house mother," made sure all guests behaved themselves, within reason. She was friendly enough, and weary with the look of someone whose forgiveness could be bought with a carton of Marlboros, or less, for the right bloke.

Stage and band in The Gamle Christiania Oslo ,Norway

The Gamle Christiania featured a nice old bar and a fairly large dining room with a wide stage that curved around one side of the dance floor. On the stage were the guitar amplifiers, drums, and the PA system with small monitors that all the bands used. We ran the mix ourselves, mainly just for the vocals. The setup was definitely adequate, except for one little logistical thing. To get onto the stage, you had to either climb over or duck under a metal and wood railing that ran along the front edge from wall-to-wall, without any step-up or opening. I guess Norwegians thought that American cowboys were used to swinging a boot up to mount their horses, unless the horse ran off with his wife like the old joke used to go. That first night I was a little apprehensive as I "mounted" the stage and started the show. I really wanted to get it right. After our first couple of songs I mentioned to the audience that we play tunes by more obscure artists like Jerry Jeff Walker, Bobby Bare, and Guy Clark . . . when someone in the audience hollered out "Guy Clark." Mentally, I let out a big sigh of relief - we were in!

Many older American country artists frequently toured overseas and the music we played was pretty much what our new audience wanted to hear. It was love-at-first-gig! We quickly learned that like our fans back home, country music fans over here liked to drink - a lot. They loved to dance too, and I mean dance wildly. That's when we realized what that railing was really for. The stage was a couple of feet tall, and the top of the railing was at roughly the same height as someone's head on the dance floor. Sometimes they'd swing their partner a little too wide and accidentally bounce their noggin off that metal and wood rail. We sure had a good laugh the first few times we felt the vibration from the impact, but after a while it was just part of the gig. An occasional goose egg didn't deter anyone from dancing and to my knowledge no additional brain damage was caused, so we just played on.

It took the first couple of nights to get things "dialed in" and then we quickly became comfortable playing at Gamle Christiania. In a way, there was practically no difference between entertaining the folks back home, and those here. In other ways, things were very different. The Norwegian authorities had public drinking under control. All of the live music venues were in a central part of downtown Oslo. This allowed the authorities (militaristic police who patrolled the streets in pairs) to keep peace with boots on the ground. Practically no one drove a car when they went out for the night. Most folks either walked or used the public transportation system that runs on electric power from overhead lines like American trolleys and streetcars of the 1920s and 30s.

Urtegata 31 is, as the crow flies, less than a mile from the Gamle Christiania, so we walked to work most nights. We began noticing on our walks back that drunk Norwegians were not too particular about where they peed when nature called. It was not unusual to see a girl step off the sidewalk into a shadow or nook, squat, pee, and then rejoin the pack, no problem. It was easy to tell when you were walking down a sidewalk where a guy had heeded the call. Sometimes we would see a continuous zig-zag line of pee left by someone who apparently just kept on walking. We got used to it and even played Hopscotch with the day-old, dried-on pee lines. Of course, there was a good reason for people to be stumbling home at that hour in that condition. If you were caught driving under the influence you lost your driver's license for two years and did some time in the calaboose. If it happened a second time, you did two years in jail and lost your driving privileges for life. Those, my friends, are some serious deterrents to drinking and driving. We soon adopted the pee-where-you-stand policy ourselves under cover of darkness on late-night jaunts. Like they say, when in Rome . . .

We were all a little wrung-out as we made our way through the streets of downtown Osla back to Urtegata 31 after that first show. The lodging was actually pretty good considering that we each had our own private rooms. Some were fairly "roomy" while others were not. I think mine was one of the smallest. You had to step out into the hallway to change your mind. Seriously, I'm talking about a space 6 feet by 8 feet, with one window. I remember thinking, I traveled across a freaking ocean to sleep in a room the size of a jail cell on a bed that makes an Army cot look nice. It seems that while I was handling some administrative issues the other four members of the band had scoped out and claimed some of the bigger rooms for themselves. That was fine with me, but what I didn't realize how thin the walls were, and that my room was next to a guy who obviously had a willing girlfriend in the band. Thank God for the headphones and a sound machine that emitted white noise I had brought along to help me sleep.

CHAPTER 17

GETTING A GRIP

There was much to learn about Oslo. After I had settled into my closet disguised as a bedroom, I went out exploring the area in hopes of finding a liquor store. I soon discovered there were none, per se. I saw a tobacco shop and thought they might also sell spirits. The young Pakistani man working there didn't have a clue about what I was looking for, nor did he seem to understand the word "bourbon" or anything else I said. I sure didn't speak Norwegian. For those who haven't seen the Norse language in print, they have words that are as long as a sentence, and sentences that are as long as a paragraph, and paragraphs that are as long as a page. You get the idea . . . Anyway, I kept looking around when there, right in plain sight, lined up in several rows, were little bottles labeled rum, gin, scotch, and voila, whiskey! Desperate, I reckoned a couple of "airplane bottles" would have to do. Great, I thought - my first purchase in a foreign city is airplane bottles of whiskey.

Back in the room, I took a little sip. It certainly was NOT whiskey. It tasted more like whiskey concentrate - definitely not something you would want to chug down. Later I found out that "liquor" stores were appropriately called the "Wine Monopoly," where a fifth of Jim Beam was about $90 American. The Norwegian government controlled the sales of all alcoholic beverages, at quite a markup. The local residents who couldn't afford these prices had adopted a familiar old "work around". They made hooch distilled from potatoes and then drank it "straight" or added some flavoring from those - you guessed it - little airplane bottles to make it taste like the beverage of their choice. Live and learn.

The weather during those first weeks in Oslo was nothing to write home about. Snow and overcast skies made many days gloomy and uninviting. At first I spent most of my free time indoors as Jim and Scooter began finding their way around the city by day. After the gig we spent our late nights partying back at Urtegata 31 or occasionally checking out the competition at other Oslo nightclubs, such as the Smuget and the Ritterhallen. By far, the best part of hanging out at Urtegata 31 was carrying on with the other musicians who shared our digs. Many of them were from around the UK, with some from other European countries such as Hungary and Italy, as well as Sweden. No surprise that we all got along famously, musicians will do that because our experiences making music were basically the same, on either side of the Atlantic. Most of them spoke fluent English, and those who didn't knew the words to most American rock and roll songs better than I did. Many of the performers played acoustic guitar, but there were some pianists, as well as drummers, bass players, even a horn or two. We all spoke the international language of music, and we took part in some amazing late-night jams downstairs in the communal dining room and kitchen.

Every morning at Urtegata 31 the kitchen opened early for breakfast. Everyone was on their own when it came to cooking eggs and omelettes, but some of us avoided the kitchen chaos in favor of coffee and cereal with milk. Every evening a hired cook would whip up a basic hot dish like spaghetti or some kind of meat-and-potato mystery. The food was actually not terrible - and it was free - though the meals weren't always true to form. One evening we had hamburgers, but the meat definitely wasn't what an American like me would consider beef. I went to the kitchen and asked the cook what we were eating. "Ham-a-blurger," he said in mangled English.

"What kind of meat are these 'ham-a-blurgers' made of?," I asked.

"Reindeer," he said. Where's a Mickey D's when you need one?

Another memorable feature of Urtegata 31 was the ever-present group of dope sniffing street people nearby. They'd sit on the sidewalk and pour paint thinner on a piece of rope and then inhale or "huff" the fumes until they were red-faced and high as a weather balloon. Sometimes when we'd exit the building these crazies would begin walking towards us babbling utter, brain-fried gibberish. They would try to keep up with our pace, but once we were onto a more visible street where the police could nab them they scurried back to their respective gutters.

CHAPTER 18

HERE COMES THE SUN

We were well into our Norwegian experience when April brought a refreshing breath of spring to Oslo. The constant clouds finally cleared out for a little sunshine and a few warm breezes, allowing us to crank open the window in our dank rooms and let some soft fresh air in. Some of us became enamoured with the city and it's amazing sights, like the Vigeland Sculpture Park, Holmenkollen with its massive Olympic ski jump, and the harbor where early in the morning fishing boats brought in the night's catch, and they sold fresh shrimp with the heads and antennae intact right on the docks. We were smoking Norwegian cigarettes (Prince brand) and generally digging Oslo's cool urban culture.

By then we were all well-known to the folks who partied at the Gamle Christiania, and they fully accepted us into their community. American men definitely had good "market value" as far as the opposite sex was concerned. Most of the Norwegian women we met at the club and elsewhere were attractive, friendly, and disarmingly down-to-earth. A couple of band members found intimate companionship and fell in love with local women they met at the club (more on that later). Daniel flew his girlfriend Jan to Oslo to join him for the second half of our engagement. I communicated with Jackie as often as I could from the one pay phone in the hallway by the front door of Urtegata

31. She was always on my mind, and I was concerned with what was going on back home and whether we'd still have any gigs. There were return dates already on the books, with another summer of juicy work to look forward to, but I guess I was getting homesick.

Monday was our one night off, and sometimes we'd go watch the local band that played at Gamle Christiania each week to give us a rest. I had never seen a more decked-out country band in my life! These guys were dressed to the hilt with kerchiefs, over-feathered hats, big rodeo belt buckles, fancy boots, the whole nine yards. If there had been a store selling Nudie suits in Oslo these guys would have been their best customers. They played really well, but It was strange to hear them sing country songs with a thick Norwegian accent. "Mamas don't let you babies glow up to be Calla-boys," and "I turned 21 in prison doing life with-oot parole, but Mama taa-ride, Mama taa-ride, Mama taa-ride"

It sure sounded different to me, and in between tunes they spoke Norwegian over the mic, so I had absolutely no idea what - or who - they were talking about.

Clinton, still the best-dressed member of our band, realized there was money to be made selling authentic, American western-style clothing. Regular old Levis jeans were hard to find over there. He went through all the clothes he'd brought along and picked out a small inventory of things he decided he could live without. Then he arranged them - with price tags - in front of his pedal steel guitar on stage at the club. His gently used items sold well. Clinton was determined to enrich himself as much as he could before the gig was over, so to clear out his last few items he slashed prices and had a sale. It's a wonder he didn't go home in cowboy boots and a barrel. The rest of us thought of selling some stuff too, but we didn't want to turn the stage into a yard sale! Besides clothes, I reckon we didn't have much to sell that we hadn't already given away for free.

Not all of our new Norwegian fans were women. A die-hard, dedicated male fan who truly adored us was Uvo. He was always smiling, and seemed to be a happy guy, who mostly hung out by himself. Like most folks over there, Uvo was very likeable and friendly, and Daniel became his buddy. He'd come to the club wearing an Elvis costume or cowboy outfits, and was always seated in the front row before we started playing. Uvo stayed to the end, drinking just water, or soda. He just loved American country music, and Americans who played it well. Another Norwegian guy who was at the club to see us nearly every night was Harold, which sounds like "harr-rolled" pronounced over there. Harold had wheels - serious wheels - a big, 1970s-vintage Chrysler sedan he made into a limousine that comfortably seated eight people. Harold was a very nice, popular fellow who was extremely friendly to our band.

Not all of the musical friends we made at Urtegata 31 were there for the whole time we were. Acts came and went according to their contracts. If no one was in the mood for jamming, we played cards, including a game called Acey Deucy or Between The Sheets that I will never play again in my life. I'm not a big gambler, but this card game is downright sneaky. For those who have not played it - don't!

Stay with me here. The player to the left of the dealer is first to act. The dealer deals two cards face up on the table (leaving some space between the two). The player places a wager based on the perceived strength of their hand. The bet may be any amount of money between the minimum bet and the amount in the pot. The player designates any "aces" in the hand as being either high (above a king) or low (below a two). After the wager is placed, a third card is dealt between the other two. If this card's rank falls between the ranks of the other two, the player wins and is paid from the pot. If the third card's rank is not in between the other two, the player loses and pays the pot. Note that matching one of the end cards, called hitting the post, is merely a painful loss. If two consecutive cards are turned up, the player forfeits the minimum bet to the pot. If a pair is turned up, the player is immediately paid two times the minimum bet. Play continues clockwise with each player taking their turn and the cards are reshuffled after the dealer's turn. Game play continues until a player takes the whole pot. Between The Sheets has a tendency to suck money into the pot at an alarmingly high rate. Therefore, if everyone agrees that they've had enough, the game can be ended by equally splitting the pot.

This one particular game had been going on for quite a while, and I was on a run of bad luck with about a month's pay in losses and the last thing I wanted to do was split the pot. The turns went around and the pot had not been won for a while. I was sweating out each turn, while rehearsing in my head how I would explain to Jackie why I came back with less money than we had planned. Well, it seemed like forever, but finally the pot was big enough to recoup my losses and it came back around to me. I recall the cards were a King and a Nine. I had to bet the pot. I held my breath as the dealer turned over… A JACK! I scooped up the money and quit playing. Truth be known I think everyone in the game was hoping that I would win. From then on I stuck with Solitaire.

CHAPTER 19

RUSSIAN RAIN IN GOD'S COUNTRY

After playing for appreciative, beer-drinking and dancing crowds at the Gamle Christiania Tuesday through Sunday for seven weeks, we finally came down to the last week of our engagement. It seemed like ages since we arrived. Our new friends and fans knew we'd soon be gone, and there was a tinge of sadness in the air as we counted down those last nights. Everyone was excited at the prospect of a return engagement. Almost everyone.

On that last Saturday night in April while walking to the Gamle Christiania I experienced a most peculiar meteorological phenomenon. Dark clouds had returned and it was raining light but steady. Jim and Scooter, and Clinton, with a plastic rain cover on his cowboy hat, and rubbers on his boots were walking with me. We noticed that the viscosity of the rain was kinda heavy and oily, unlike anything I had seen before. To me it was almost kinda soupy looking. I swear it wasn't my imagination - there was definitely something strange about the rain that night. At the time we dismissed it as just another strange thing among many on this trip. When we got back to Urtegata 31 after the gig someone told us the news that Chernobyl had melted down that day. We were about 200 miles - more or less as the crow flies - from the disaster site and the plume of the radioactive cloud, according to the next morning's paper, came directly over Oslo.

Russian rain in God's country

To this day I remember how different the rain felt that night, and I hope to never feel rain like that again.

Before we left Oslo, Harold, our friend from the club with the Chrysler limo, took the band and a few close friends of ours on an incredible trip to Lillehammer up at the northern tip of the Mjosa Fjord. This was the first actual road trip outside of Oslo any of us had been on since we arrived. It was especially nice to have Harold as our experienced driver who knew his way around so all we had to do was sit back and enjoy the ride. Once we were well outside the city limits, the countryside was a spectacular series of mountains, hills, forests, and fjords. Harold drove us through some of the quaint little towns along the shores of the Mjosa fjord, and we stopped at a cafe somewhere where we sat outside and took in the stunning panoramic views. I thought of all those American beer commercials that use the great outdoors as a backdrop. I also think at that moment we all reflected a little on our time in Norway, and the different experiences we had.

This gig had been one hell of an interesting ride, but frankly I didn't see any future for me here. We could have probably played the Gamle Christiania a couple of times a year if we wanted to, because our gig had definitely been a success and they were ready to give us another date. I didn't see how that was going to make us a better band going forward though, or help us get a record deal, or enable us to open for bigger and better headliners in the States. I was well aware that band members with new love interests were obviously anxious to come back, but I was so ready to be home with Jackie at that point that I just couldn't imagine being away from her that long again anytime soon. When we all got on the plane to go home, I knew there would be no return trip. It's a decision I've not regretted, and like all decisions, there were consequences.

Chapter 20
SWEET HOME MILWAUKEE

I was very much looking forward to some much-needed rest (among other things) when we touched down in the good old U.S.A. Although we had played a lot in Milwaukee, six nights a week for eight weeks running was more than any of us had worked in recent memory. Some well-earned days off were in order before we resumed our club gigs. It was early spring, and another season of festival gigs and other good work was in the offing. Friends and fans were genuinely glad to have us back, and we regaled them with tales of our Norwegian exploits and the folks we met over there. After relating the story of the radioactive rain from Chernobyl, I thought of pulling a joke on our audience where each of us in the band would have one of those green glowsticks strategically placed in our pants. With the lights up I'd mention the rain story, then the lights would go off to reveal each member - literally - glowing in the dark. Never did it though.

Not long after our return from Oslo we taped a performance of two songs for a locally-produced television special called "Studio 12." The production was done at Breezeway Studio in Waukesha, and it was cool to be back where we had recently recorded our album. The tunes we laid down for the video cameras were Hoyt Axton's "Idol Of The Band" and "Fool In The Mirror" by Guy Clark. The band was as tight as we had ever been, and the multi-camera setup the producer used nicely captured the energy of the band and the interplay of the lead instruments with the rhythm section. Along with our two contributions, the program also featured performances by such prominent Milwaukee acts as Jack Grassell, Leroy Airmaster, and John Seiger's Semi-Twang. Pretty good company, I'd say! The show aired on Friday, August 8th, 1986, on Milwaukee Channel 12 at 9 p.m. I know that because I kept a copy of the TV Guide with the listing.

That summer we played more church festivals than hot beads on a rosary. Here's a partial list of the ones I remember: St. Albert's, St. Sylvester, Immaculate Heart of Mary, St. Agnes, Our Mother Of Perpetual Help, Our Lady of Good Hope, Our Lady of Good Luck (just seeing if you're still paying attention), and the list goes on. We also played a thing called Mitchell Street Days in Milwaukee's old blue collar neighborhood on the near south side where we were reminded of how events like this get you in front of audiences you don't play for anywhere else and, observing the parade of misfits and "beauties" on Mitchell Street that afternoon, we were glad that was true. Most were older women with more children than Mother Hubbard, and one guy wore a tee-shirt with skulls and flags on it that said "Kill 'em all, let God sort 'em out." We also played downtown for Bastille Days, and Polishfest at the lakefront.

At Summerfest we opened for Greg Allman and Dickey Betts, two of the baddest Southern rockers around. Allman kept a glass of water on top of his keyboards to dip his fingers into throughout the show. My band was in a peculiar situation because Clinton had very recently injured his wrist and was temporarily out-of-commission. Rather than making Jim play all the solos (of which there were many) I hired Jason Klagstad, an ace guitarist who played in one of my favorite local country bands, Plumb Loco. Pretty much every time I'd go out to see them play they'd invite me up on stage and roll into "Ain't Livin' Long Like This." I like the song and they played it great, but in a key that was a little high for my range. They'd just start it and give me the nod, before I could ask them to drop the key. I really had to stretch to sing the chorus and hold those long notes . . . It wasn't my best work, but I tried.

Jim and Jason made a mighty lead guitar duo, with different sounds and playing styles- except that it almost didn't happen. Before we went on, Jason was looking for something in his gear bag when he ran his left index finger into a nut saw he carried (for making or enlarging slots in a guitar's nut - the little thing at the top of the neck that the strings go through) and cut it wide open. With blood spurting, he remembered something he had read about superglue and how it was originally used in battle during the Vietnam war. Holding his bleeding fingertip together, he used his other hand to apply dabs of superglue (which he also carried in his bag) to the wound. Not only did it pretty much stop the bleeding, the pain subsided in a minute or two, and he was ready to go on stage. Now there's a pro! We returned for another run at the Florian II at

Bailey's Harbor in beautiful Door County. They had a little "band trailer" for us to sleep in, and Jim brought a tent and slept outside in the cool night air.

As the gigs flew by, we were playing like clockwork and generally enjoying life as a country band-for-hire, but we were no closer to any significant recording or management deal. It's easy to get caught-up in the time-consuming business of gigging. You work your butt off to become a top act in your market, only to find out that reaching the next level of success takes a whole lot more. Mostly it takes luck, and good timing. Right time, right place, and all. We probably should have been making a new record by then, or talking about it, but we weren't. We weren't learning new songs or writing songs of our own. We were busy working, and living. Like the old blues song goes "I live the life I love and I love the life I live." When you're working alot and making good money, it's easy to become complacent. Some folks have told me I should have moved the band to Nashville, but I doubt everyone would have been up for that much of a gamble. It just wasn't a viable option.

A few weeks after the "Studio 12" TV show aired, Jim informed me that he was leaving the band. I can't say that I was completely surprised by this, but it was still a jolt. He had been with me since the beginning, and his guitar work had become a "signature" part of our sound, kinda like Don Rich with Buck Owens. I guess the way Jim saw it, the band was not progressing. Our song list had become stale for him. To top it off, he had fallen in love with a Norwegian woman who came to visit him in Milwaukee that summer. They were getting serious and the realization that the band was not going back to Oslo was probably very disappointing. Jim offered to stay on until a replacement was found, which was good because I had no idea where I was gonna find someone who played like him. It kinda felt like a door closing, but like they say, sometimes one door closes and another door opens.

Jim's departure ushered in big changes for The River Delta Band. Clinton also opted out after Jim left. Once again, it was a lot to lose. His pedal steel guitar had become as much a part of our "sound" as my own voice. This is the part of being a bandleader that sucks, frankly. Musical friendships run deep. You can't take it personally, but it kinda hurts.

Apparently I'm no stranger to good luck, though, because in a few months two new very talented players were in the lineup. Enter Joe Gorman on guitar and vocals, and George Nestler on keyboards, vocals and harmonica. Musicians bend and shape a band's musical direction with their particular expertise, and both these guys created a significant change in the band's sound, the dynamics of how we played, and the songs we chose. George's playing on the electronic keyboard and the variety of sounds he used was something the band never had before. It helped us get into some new music and put a new glimmer on the songs we'd been playing for years. Joe knew his way around an electric guitar like nobody's business.

Boy, could he play fast! His fingers flew like the wind over that fretboard. As he settled into his new musical space, I could hear him listening and adjusting his lightning-quick licks to fit what we were doing. When Joe played a solo, he animated them physically with extreme facial contortions while twisting his guitar all around. Some of our fans came up with a nickname for him - "Orgasm."

It was so different, but difference is often a good thing, and once I was used to the sonic shift I got to really liking the revised band. We now had four strong vocalists and a fresh instrumental push. We changed up our set list to include some new material while keeping some of the "standards" that our fans still loved. It definitely shook me up some, but fortunately it didn't shake the loyalty of our fans. The door that opened allowed us (hell, forced us) to update some of our material to be a little more current with mainstream country music. Believe me, this kind of thing doesn't happen easily. I tried to focus on staying true to my own musical direction as the sands shifted around me. Everybody in this business knows the importance of tweaking your brand to stay relevant. The band wasn't reinvented but it was certainly remodeled, like a good old house that needed new paint and fresh furnishings. I was now motivated to get back into the studio.

CHAPTER 21

FRESH BAND, FRESH BRAND

Earlier that year we had gotten a new corporate sponsorship with the G. Heileman Brewing Company, specifically for their brand Special Export Light. After being known for six years as "Phil Delta and The River Delta Band," it felt like less of a mouthful to just say "The Phil Delta Band." That's what most people called us anyway, so why buck the trend? It made for a better logo too that looked great on the hats, T-shirts, and other new swag Heileman printed up for us.

My plan for recording took me back to Waukesha, but this time at a new studio called Nexxus. Two excellent engineers, Jacque Sewery and Pat Lilley, had opened a place in a former industrial building, with plenty of room to set-up a whole band. We were so proud of our new sound and the enthusiastic response from fans that instead of recording guide tracks and then overdubbing everything (as we did for our LP) we recorded "live," that is, all of us playing together like we were doing a gig. Each instrument had its own track on the recorder and isolation techniques were used to prevent the instruments from bleeding (being heard) on other tracks. I brought in Jeff Shaffer, our live sound mixer, to dial in the mix on each song we recorded. Once the songs were recorded, Jacque worked his post-production engineering magic on what we had done.

We chose ten of the best songs we were playing at the time for this project. A couple of the songs from the "Studio 12" television show, "Idol Of The Band" and "Fool In My Mirror" were included, along with "Blackberry Wine" a Gordon Lightfoot song that had been on our songlist for years. Other favorite toe-tappers, "Louisiana Man" (inspired more by Dave Edmunds' version than Doug Kershaw's) and Jerry Jeff Walker's "Public Domain," were both long-time crowd favorites. On the newer side was Steve Earle's "Devil's Right Hand," which begins the tape. I was really taken with Steve's songs, his sound, and his mojo. I still am. His songwriting is powerful and honest, with a rebel edge that isn't phoney or gratuitous. To create a little contrast in tempos we recorded a Kris Kristofferson ballad "Shipwrecked in the 80s" from an album he made on Monument Records in 1983. We also threw in a very catchy tune by Chick Raines and Bill Caswell called "That's What Your Love Does To Me." The last of the ten songs we recorded was our version of Jerry Jeff's version of Guy Clark's "L.A. Freeway." Like Jerry Jeff himself might have said, it's all just public domain.

The polish of the "new" band really came off on the recording. Scooter and Daniel had now been playing together for three years of solid gigging, and they were tight. With the expertise of Joe and George, it sounded like we had been playing together for years, not months. The concept and marketing of "Live Tracks" was to sell folks at our gigs a fresh recording that sounded like we did in a club where they heard us.

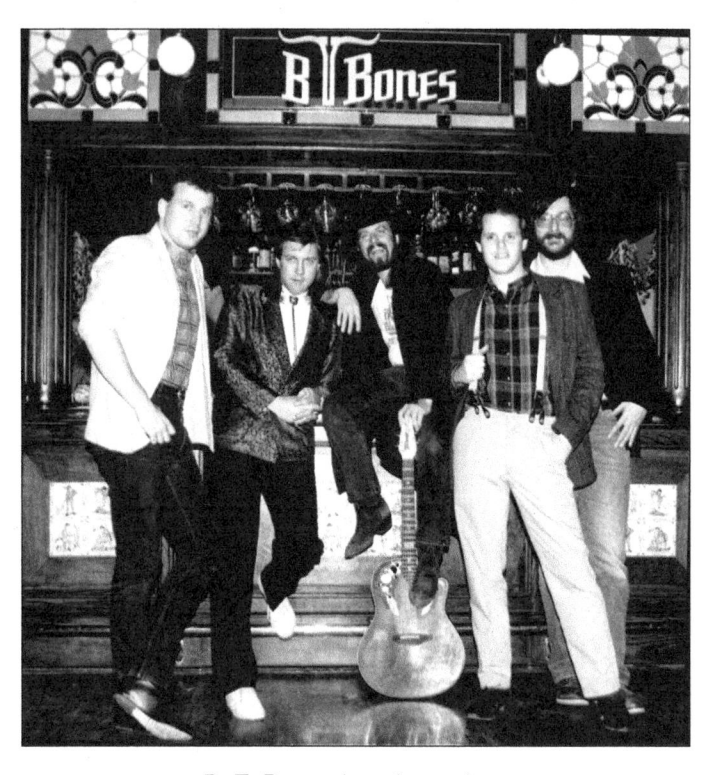

B. T. Bones band members

It worked well and we sold a bunch of cassettes. The plan was that once the production costs were repaid, the profits would be put aside to pay for our next studio recording. When the profits arrived, that is.

By the end of 1986 we were loaded for bear, and ready to take Milwaukee (and the world) by storm (again). Yet when the new year dawned, our business was changing. The popular surge of "new" country music in the wake of Urban Cowboy had just about run its course in the Beer City, home to polkas and

Laverne and Shirley. Some of the clubs we played that were doing a gangbuster business were now struggling or going down altogether. As I told the Milwaukee Journal in an interview in February, there were fewer and fewer cowboy hats in the audience. Once again, Lady Luck smiled on me when The Phil Delta Band was hired for a weekly gig at a brand new restaurant and bar called B. T. Bones. Located in the Brookfield Square shopping mall, this spacious venue looked to me like a combination of Pinnacle Peak rustic and T.G.I. Friday's razzle-dazzle. It provided us steady work to get through the winter and be sharp for another busy summer of festivals. B. T. Bones was a great home for us, with a very friendly staff who liked to have fun. Week after week we cranked out the songs on our list, but things weren't always exactly like clockwork. Being the lead singer, I tried to play each song at a speed that felt comfortable to me, which I'll admit varied depending on how I was feeling, what kind of a night it was, etc. Sometimes we'd be into a song and I'd feel it dragging, or at least at that moment it felt that way to me. To rectify the situation I would try and speed things up which occasionally drove the band crazy. One night Scooter and I got into an argument over this, and we took it to the employee locker room to have it out. I remember us both hitting the locker doors - instead of each other - as we vented our frustrations. It happens.

On another night I asked Jeff to make a cassette recording of the band directly from the mixing board so

I could review how we were playing, and what the mix was sounding like. Most soundmen have a "talk back" microphone at the mixer, so they can communicate with the band members through the monitors regarding adjustments and levels when necessary. When I played back the tape, I kept hearing a voice in the mix I hadn't heard before. After some puzzlement, I realized it was Jeff singing along with the band with his talk back mic. I couldn't hear it when we were playing because it wasn't in the monitors, but his voice was in the main speakers so everybody in the audience heard it! Jeff received a simple directive from me - NEVER sing with the band again, EVER.

As winter slowly gave way to spring, I began playing some solo gigs at B. T. Bones in addition to the nights the band played. One afternoon I was setting up my equipment and saw something I'll never forget. A crew of Internal Revenue Service agents basically stormed the place and immediately shut it down. They took all the cash out of the registers, and were proceeding to padlock the doors when I asked them - nicely - if I could please remove all my gear from the premises. "Don't shoot me, I'm just the singer!" As Forrest Gump might have said, and just like that, B. T. Bones was no more. It sure was sad to see such a nice gig disappear, especially since it was by no fault of ours.

CHAPTER 22

BLUE CHIPS AND FISH TIES

Our appearance at Summerfest with the new lineup was a success, and it came with a non-monetary bonus. I was sitting in our backstage dressing room with a couple of other band members when none other than Steve Earle, the act we were opening for, came strolling in with his guitar and sat down next to me on the couch. There he was, one of my musical heroes, up-close and personal. He was animated, and very talkative. In short order he passed on a lot of good advice, especially where your song publishing rights are concerned. Steve said original songs are like your "blue chip" stocks, and to never sell your publishing rights. He talked for quite a while about music business stuff, including a photo shoot he had booked in Germany the next day. Steve toured with over a dozen of his own guitars and a crack team of techs who brought out a different one every third or fourth song. He had a couple of killer lead guitar players in his band, too. During the show it seemed like he was constantly breaking G strings. That man really laid down some rhythm when he played!

Around that time the most listened-to country music radio station in our market, WMIL-FM, began a big fundraiser for the Prevention of Child Abuse Foundation. They set up a live broadcast on the roof of a K-Mart store with two of their top DJs, "Real Neil" Dion and Mitch Morgan. They also enlisted Milwaukee Bucks Head Coach Don Nelson to help them raise money. The idea was "Nellie" (as he was affectionately known) and the morning DJs would stay on the rooftop until the fundraising goal was met. The Phil Delta Band performed on a Saturday afternoon to kick the whole thing off. At one point Don Nelson requested "Blackberry Wine" from our Live Tracks cassette. Turns out it was one of Nellie's favorite songs, and after we finished, he handed down one of his own homemade bottles of blackberry wine to me. You may remember "fish ties," a popular novelty necktie back then. Nellie was a fan of those, too, and that day he and the DJs were all wearing one, and handing them out to folks in the audience. After we played I was invited to join them up on the roof. The first thing Nellie asked me was, "Where's your tie?" When I told him I didn't have one he promptly took off his and offered it to me. I asked him to autograph it, and he wrote a very nice thank you and signed it "Nellie - 1987." I still have that fish tie and it hangs proudly around the neck of a trophy buck I had bagged in Wisconsin a couple of years earlier.

The next week I wrote a song for this event entitled "I'm Just A Kid." For the past couple of years I had been a stepdad to Jackie's little boy Jonathan, and I was familiar with occasional parenting situations where tempers are tested. One day he spilled a whole glass of Mountain Berry Punch Kool-Aid on our brand new living room carpet. My initial reaction was to yell at him, but I didn't. I just told him that it was okay and that accidents sometimes happen (Rug Doctor to the rescue). I got to thinking about how that little bit of forgiveness created so much love and trust, and how I couldn't imagine ever lifting a finger to strike a child of my own, when I sat down and began writing these lines:

> *I'm just a kid, not even sure what I did,*
> *But was it really that bad, to make you so mad that you could hurt me?*
> *Hey, I'm just a kid, doin' things like you did;*
> *When you were my size. Please realize that I'm just a kid.*
>
> *I'm just a kid, I get in things that I shouldn't,*
> *I just have to try it, when you said that I couldn't;*
> *I always want stuff that seems to cost a lotta' money,*
> *Things crack me up, that you don't think are funny.*
>
> *And I don't mean to break things, that I break on purpose,*
> *And I try to set still when I see you're nervous;*
> *But please understand that I'm not yet a man,*
> *I'm just a kid.*
>
> *(spoken) Sorta' keep my feelin's hid.*
> *But when you swing at me.*
> *The hate that I see, I can never forget.*

And when it happens next time.
Reach way back in your mind.
To when you were my size,
Just look in these eyes . . . (spoken) I'm just a kid

I don't mean to break stuff, that I break on purpose,
And I try to set still, when I see you're nervous;
But please understand that I'm not yet a man,
I'm just a kid.

And when it happens next time,
Stop and think back in your time...
"Dad, were you ever a kid?"

When I finished the lyrics I went into the studio at Nexxus and made a simple recording of the song. After it was finished, an idea came to me. For the final touch, I took Jonathan into the studio and we recorded him saying - in his cutest little kid voice - the line "I'm just a kid" at the very end. I sent a copy to the WMIL DJs who loved it, and they asked me to bring Jonathan up to their rooftop broadcast to wave at the audience as the song was played over the radio. Jackie and I were so proud of him! It was a very memorable moment for the three of us.

Later that summer, Bucks' coach Don Nelson called on us to participate in a remarkable Farm-Aid type fundraising effort. Nellie donated his NBA playoff earnings to a Wisconsin farmer on the verge of foreclosure, and then began an eight-day tractor ride collecting money for other Wisconsin farmers in similar straits. He began his 250-mile trip at the good old State Fairgrounds (home to many Phil Delta gigs) driving a donated J.I. Case tractor with a trailer hauling a giant piggy bank. He named the bank Barkley, after Charles Barkley. Miller Brewing kicked in $40,000 to get things rolling, and Nellie pledged to lose fifty pounds on his ride (he sure knew how to raise money). WMIL had recorded our band performing our version of Merle Haggard's "Amber Waves Of Grain" and was playing it on the air to promote Nellie's Farm Fund as it was officially called. He finished his ride in Wausau, so we drove up there to put on a show for Nellie and his many supporters. Too bad this was the dead middle of August. For those who may be unaware, the middle of Wisconsin in August can be as hot and stifling as the Mississippi Delta. It was so hot that day, we could see the folding chairs set up in the parking lot sinking into the asphalt. We never actually played.

Like every other summer since I started this band, the festivals and gigs flew by as the end of the "season" snuck up on us. This time it also brought yet another personnel change. After putting in three terrific years on bass guitar, Daniel decided to quit the band and leave Wisconsin. His playing, singing, and stage presence were gonna be hard to replace. With demand for our kind of modern country music now at a low, it would be hard to find someone local to put in the time and effort to keep the band as tight as we had finally gotten it. Like I've said, the one thing you can count on in this business is that things will change.

It just so happened that a guy from Texas named Ron Garrett was married to a Milwaukee woman who wanted to be back home for a while. Ron played bass and guitar, and sang like a bird. On some tunes, Ron could out-sing me, plus he could yodel. So there I was, competing with a yodeler - again! He'd played in bands around his home state, mostly in Austin and Amarillo. Ron was recently in a group called Texas Suburban and had opened for many of the songwriters I loved. He had found a day job, but he wanted to keep playing with a band on the level he had been doing back home. Once again, the grapevine among Milwaukee music stores led him to me. For the very first time, I wasn't the only actual Southerner in the group! It looked like "the beginning of beautiful friendship," like Claude Raines says to Bogie in the closing scene of Casablanca.

Chapter 23

ELVIS WANTS TO LEAVE THE BUILDING

One night Ron and I went out clubbing, to get better acquainted over drinks and check out the competition. After being out on the prowl and having WAY too much to drink we decided to go see one of Milwaukee's local Elvis impersonators, G. L. Wesley, who had checked out a number of our performances over the years, had sat-in with us a few times. G. L. was a nice guy and he did a convincing impersonation of the mega-star and musical hero who resided in my hometown of Memphis Tennessee. Ron and I drank our way through his set, and he gave me a little wave of acknowledgement as we paddled down the ol' Whiskey River. At break time I asked him to join us at our table. "Well, thankya'ver-much Phil," he said in his best Elvis voice. As we exchanged pleasantries I realized that G. L. did not break character - he used "Elvispeak" during the whole conversation as if it was perfectly normal. Ron and I glanced at each other trying not to laugh at this offstage act. The club owner brought us a couple more drinks (on Elvis, I mean G. L.) which we definitely did not need. Before hitting the stage again, he asked us if we'd like to come up and do a song. I said we would love to. It was a bad decision.

After a couple of tunes, G. L. announced that a good friend of his is in the "arena" tonight and he'd like him to come up and do a song. "Ladies and Genamen, I'd like to invita' great friend'a mine up, Mr. Phil

Delta" With that nice intro I went on up and asked everybody "to please welcome a new member of The Phil Delta Band to join me, Ron Garrett" Ron joined me and we had a quick huddle, during which I said "Hell, I don't think I know all the words to any Elvis song. What are we gonna do?" Ron was in the same drunken condition as me, so no help from him. We quickly asked the band if they could play any of our songs . . . crickets. With the clock ticking I blurted to Ron "Let's do 'Memphis.'" I thought for sure an Elvis impersonator's band would know the song named for the city where the man himself had lived so I turned to the band and said, "Y'all know Memphis don't you?" . . . crickets. "You know, Da . . . Da . . . Da . . . Da-Da-Da, Da . . . Da . . . Da . . . Da-Da-Da" . . . more crickets. Caught by surprise, feeling some pressure, and being highly intoxicated, I grabbed the microphone and said, "Let's do one for Elvis' hometown... Memphis!"

I told the band the song is just two chords - G and D - and to just stay on G between verses. Rather than trying to teach the guitarist the Lonnie Mack lick that opens and closes the song, Ron and I just sang it and again tried not to laugh at the absurd situation we were in. I sang the first verse:

Long distance information give me Memphis, Tennessee
Help me find the party trying to get in touch with me
She did not leave her number, but I know who placed the call

> *'Cause my uncle took the message and he wrote it on the wall*

I searched long and hard in my inebriated brain for the words to the second verse but came up short, so I sang the first verse again because I had to sing something. "Long distance information give me Memphis, Tennessee . . . " When the third verse came around Ron nudged me away from the mic and said "I got this" Then he sang the words to the first verse again! "Long distance information give me Memphis, Tennessee . . . " With that we were both laughing our asses off, right there on stage. I waved for the band to end the damn song, and then said with a drunken slur, "Thankya'ver-much." Ron and I hightailed it out of that bar laughing so hard we had tears when we reached the door. Needless to say G. L. Wesley never invited me to sing with his band again, mainly because I never showed up at his performances anymore. I still chuckle every time I hear "Memphis."

In October we started a regular gig at a club with two levels called Starz on 100 (first floor) and Beneath the Starz (guess where). Starz ran rock and pop acts upstairs, with country down below. Ron brought a distinct twang and a whole different presence to the stage. He was no stranger to country music, and you sure could hear it in his singing and playing. Throughout the fall and into another winter the band played every week and looked forward to the possibilities ahead. We were talking about recording a new single at a studio in Chicago, and pedaling it to every country radio station where we might get a foot in the door. Maybe we could get an agent to shop us to a record label. The agent and the label would probably get all the money, but at least we might get to the next level as an act. Some people were getting very rich in this business, and I sure wouldn't have minded being one of them, but that's not really why I started a band. Like the joke goes, I didn't get into music to make a lot of money, and so far it's worked out really well.

Chapter 24

THE REAL MR. GOODWRENCH

When I look back on all our experiences playing music for people, the aforementioned band bus I drove for many thousands of miles looms large in those memories. If there is a heaven for band buses our 'ol trouper is certainly resting there. If she could talk, she'd have many tales to tell of tenacity, trickery, and various conjugal acts that won't be described in this book! I bought her from Gary Zimmerman, leader of "The Lost Armadillo Desert Band" another one of my favorite Milwaukee country groups at the time. She was never officially given a name, but had she ever been christened, it certainly would NOT have been "Old Dependable." "Mysterious" or "Uncertain" would have been more apt. She was certainly a welcome refuge from the festival crowds, or on those night gigs when a band member needed a place to make out or sleep off a little too much whiskey. As for consistently making it down the road, well that's another story.

For almost a year she had a mysterious problem of running along just fine when outta' the blue the motor would stop and start running again within a few seconds. This was the strangest thing I had ever experienced with any motor vehicle. Fortunately, one of our favorite fans, our buddy Don Stewart, was a professional auto mechanic. "Stew" as we called him, was definitely a wiz with the wrenches and if he couldn't fix it, by God it was time to get another one. Stew was my first phone call when this random starting-and-stopping-syndrome beset the bus, and he instructed me to bring her over to Ruby Chevrolet, the dealership where he worked. A dozen or so mechanics - many of them fans of our band - worked in the big garage there, and they tended to go easy on me when writing up the repair bill.

Before Stew and the crew could begin working on her, the bus had to be jacked-up and pushed into a spot where she didn't block the path of other cars in for repair. The garage was for cars and regular-sized passenger trucks. A vehicular beast her size looked like the giant from "Gulliver's Travels" next to those shiny Impalas, Malibus, and Blazers. Damn, what is this going to cost? was my first thought as I watched dang near every employee in the garage put their diagnostic skills to work. Mechanics (and their supervisors) don't work cheap, and after hours of examination, they couldn't find anything wrong. Stew broke the news to me and said he'd try to solve the mystery with me at my house next time. When I asked him what I owed them for the day's work, Stew waved me off. "We couldn't find the problem and the boss man likes your music, so no charge." As I drove her home I remember thinking, ain't it great to have such good fans?

Stew came over on a very cold Saturday (imagine that in Wisconsin), and started his own long and winding road of engine analysis, with me in tow. We started working on her early while the winter sun was still providing a smidgen of warmth. I endured the cold as

Stew and Me Celebrate Bus Repair

his inept mechanical side-kick who probably got in the way more than anything, but Stew and I were - and still are - the best of friends. Besides, I like being around guys who aren't scared to get their hands greasy or bust a knuckle now and then. After several hours under the hood and all around and under that dang bus we took a break to thaw our frozen extremities inside the warm house. Stew quizzed me on situations when the ol' girl would start missing and then start back running while rolling down the road. After a few beers and much mechanical pondering he finally said, "There's only one thing else I can think of to do. We got to pull the gas tank" Gee, that sounded like fun - not! So back out we went.

I was as good at open heart surgery as I was at removing a gas tank on a bus, but Stew knew what to do. We maneuvered the tank every which way, and we shone a flashlight inside looking for any kind of clue. About the time we were about to give up for the day, we gave the tank innards one more look with the flashlight when Stew said "Wait . . . I SEE SOMETHING!" We started fishing down the throat of the gas tank with anything long and skinny - extended screwdrivers and other lengthy tools. Finally Stew used a long piece of twisted wire to remove the culprit. It was the strip of cardboard from the opening of a 12-pack of beer! How in the hell it ever got in there, and when, is still a mystery, but Stew quickly figured out exactly what was going on. That cardboard strip had a thin plastic coating on one side that kept it from breaking down and dissolving in the gasoline. He explained that the gas line feeding the engine runs down to within about a half inch of the bottom of the tank, so you can drive until it's practically empty. Every time the tank got low that pesky cardboard strip would be sucked-up against the gas line opening, which temporarily blocked the fuel supply to the engine, making it sputter. When the engine stopped, the suction on the gas line also stopped which released the strip blocking the opening, and the flow of gas to the motor resumed. So, just like that, the mystery was solved and the ol' bus was running fine again, thanks to Stew. I should have saved that stupid cardboard 12-pack strip some idiot put in there, but in my joy and relief of having the problem solved I threw that sucker away! Jackie took a picture that I still have of Stew, my mechanic hero, and myself standing in front of the bus toasting our success with a can of very cold beer.

CHAPTER 25
GOOD THINGS COME IN LARGE PACKAGES

One of the coolest gigs we played besides Summerfest happened on March 12, 1988 at a place called Zivko's Ballroom. I like to say that's when The Charlie Daniels Band "closed the show" for us (wink, wink). Charlie Daniels had scored major hits in the 1970s, and even ten years later you couldn't go anywhere without hearing "The Devil Went Down To Georgia" on the jukebox or covered by a live country band. Zivko's, out in Hartford, Wisconsin, was a grand old dance hall that had hosted some of the biggest names in popular music since the late 1940s. With a huge stage and dance floor, it was a great-sounding hall to play in. The Charlie Daniels Band was a big deal of a show at Zivko's Ballroom.

We were the first load-in, and got everything in place pretty quickly. For shows like this a large PA system is furnished, so it was a quick, painless setup. Charlie's buses arrived just before we started our sound check and although he stayed on his bus (typical with most stars), his personal manager, his band and crew came in to check out the room, and the opening act - us.

After our soundcheck I was standing by the soundboard which was setup near the middle of the floor. A thirty-some young man with a laminated pass hanging around his neck walked up, introduced himself, and mentioned that we sounded great. I took the flattery, thanked him, and offered to help with anything he needed. His compliment tarnished a bit when he said, "Well, maybe you can help me out. Do you know where I could get some weed?" I was caught a little off guard and after an awkward pause I said no, I couldn't help him but that relief was likely in the offing when more people arrived. My assurance didn't console him much.

The best thing that came out of that show was a result of both good karma and happenstance. In the audience was Bill Davidson, Jr., a good fan of The Phil Delta Band. He was there with his dad, "Willie G." Davidson, an employee of Harley Davidson Motor Company since 1963 and then head honcho of the Willie G. Davidson Product Development Center in Wauwatosa. Willie G. liked Charlie Daniels and apparently he liked us that night, too. Bill Jr. found me in the dressing room backstage after our set and invited me to meet his dad. Are you kidding? "It would be an honor," I told him. The personification of an ultra-cool biker, decked out in his trademark cap, black leather, and silver jewelry, Willie G. designed such iconic Harley bikes as the Super Glide and the Low Rider. We had a great talk until Charlie Daniels came on and we had to shout over the PA. Willie G. and Bill Jr. of course had ringside seats.

A few days later Bill, Jr. called and asked me to meet him for lunch. He said that after we played Willie's comment to him was we were a "damned good local band." When he asked if I would like to be sponsored by Harley Davidson, it didn't take me long to answer. Are you kidding? Yes! We still had our deal with G. Heileman Special Export Light, but since this wasn't another beer company there'd be no conflict of interest so I figured two sponsorships were better than one (well, duh!). Besides, it was Harley friggin' Davidson!!! That's how Harley-Davidson Motor Company became my fifth and final sponsor. The icing on this particular cake was I had just "automatically" landed a bunch of biker gigs for the band. Usually biker gigs were great. Everybody was cool and having fun, rarely sober and regularly stoned, and where there were bikers there were biker chicks. Scantily-clad, uninhibited women, riding on the shoulders of their biker boyfriends at concerts, had a tendency to regularly show-off their bare breasts. We weren't used to such competition for attention onstage . . . but we got over it!

A sad footnote to this story is Charlie Daniels' recent passing. He lived in Mount Juliet, Tennessee not very far - as the crow flies - across Old Hickory Lake from where I live today.

Chapter 26

SMOKE 'EM IF YOU GOT 'EM REDUX

The Phil Delta Band was sounding great and plugging right along, but our plans for recording a new single in a big studio were still just plans. The Live Tracks cassette had sold pretty well at first, but sales had tapered off considerably. When I heard about another Marlboro Talent Roundup, this time in the Chicago-area, I was interested.

With my revamped, hot band I figured I had a damned good chance of doing well, and maybe even winning again, so say the dreams - I would at least give it a try, though I'll admit there were two things that I didn't fully consider. Number one was the rule that at least one band member had to live in the state where the contest was held. The second thing was the judges - locally selected individuals who might be predisposed to vote for a locally favored contestant.

Somewhere along the way I met a great keyboardist who lived in Chicago named Scott May. Scott was a sales rep for The Hammond Organ Company who not only had exceptional chops, but was a great singer too. Working for Hammond, Scott always played the latest and the greatest keyboard models the company offered. George graciously agreed to temporarily step out of the lineup on keys so Scott could play the contest with us and make it "legal."

By this time Clinton had come back "into the fold" because he missed playing pedal steel, but for some

Scott May and the Chicago Band at Summerfest

reason he couldn't make it to the initial round of playoffs. Scott designed a "patch" on his keyboard that not only sounded like a pedal steel, but he could actually "bend" the notes with a pitch wheel similar to what Clinton did with the foot pedals and knee levers on his instrument. With my eyes closed I could hardly tell the difference. That's how Scott May became a member of The Phil Delta Band. Normally I wouldn't do this, but I asked him to send in the contest entry form along with the fee (to make it look good), and he was pleasantly surprised to receive an overnight envelope on his doorstep the next morning with my reimbursement. He called me up and said, "Man, you run this band better than most businesses!" which made me feel good and a little proud that he recognized that.

Someone, I forget who, began referring to Scott as our "FIB" player. When he heard the comment, Scott thought it meant we were using him to "fib" about us being an Illinois band. He later found out that "FIB" is a longstanding Wisconsin reference to Chicago residents as "f**king Illinois bastards." He took it in jest and still tells that story today. Like the Milwaukee contest we won four years earlier, there were thirty local bands in the initial play-off, with ten bands each at three Chicago-area clubs. Here's where the next bus story comes in.

"She" was once again out of commission for that first round of the Chicago Marlboro Talent Roundup. Now that we were all signed-up legal, we had to make that gig I had long ago sold my old pickup truck and bought a car after we acquired the band bus. I had no other vehicle to haul equipment with, so I called around to everyone I knew, with no luck. I was starting to panic when I looked outside and saw my good friend and next door neighbor, Terry Krajcik, a long haul trucker who had just brought home a trailer attached to his truck cab. The trailer was about a hundred times bigger than our band equipment but Terry - being the amazing friend of the band that he was - agreed to haul the gear down there and back for us. When we loaded the gear into his trailer, It sorta' looked like one potato in a 50 lb. potato sack. We had to use every bungee cord we could find to tie all the equipment together and then lash it to the wall to keep it from bouncing around inside this giant, still mostly empty box. When we arrived at the venue, the other bands we were competing against surely did a double-take as this huge tractor trailer rig pulled up just like a big-time act they might be opening for someday. Maybe it was even a little prophetic, since we won the first play-off round.

The finals were held at a Holiday Inn in Arlington Heights that had a huge nightclub named Feathers, complete with a giant aviary across the entire back wall of the venue. I guessed the caged birds were mostly deaf from all the loud music. It was a huge space, with a big stage, a spacious dance floor, and tons of seating. We played really well in that final contest round, and we came in at second place, behind a local favorite. As it turned out it was Scott's pedal steel keyboard patch that worked against us. It sounded so realistic that the judges actually called us out for playing with a recording of a pedal steel guitar! Scott invited the judges up to the stage where he demonstrated what they were hearing was indeed not a recording. They got kinda embarrassed about it, which likely did not weigh in our favor. It was a disappointment, to be sure, but the management at Feathers was impressed enough to offer us an ongoing five night-a-week gig. The pay was good, audiences were great, drinks were free and we each got our own nightly hotel room, including our new sound man, Kermit. Some band members commuted back to their day jobs in Milwaukee most nights while the rest of us hung out in Chicago all week.

Chapter 27

WHAT A LONG, STRANGE TRIP IT'S BEEN

The final bus story began when I offered it for sale with a classified ad in the local papers (yes, pre-internet, we actually had to pay for little ads in the newspaper to sell stuff). I really didn't need the cantankerous (emphasis on tank) old beast anymore, and the buyer I found was quite an interesting guy. He said he drove to Arkansas several times a year to mine for quartz crystals, which he fashioned into jewelry and sold at Grateful Dead concerts. He definitely seemed like a "Dead head." He didn't have enough money to pay for the bus in full, but he had about half the price in cash. I liked the guy, and I appreciated that he was fanatical about music. I really needed to unload the bus once and for all, so I agreed to do owner financing so he could buy it and put it to good use. I drew up a hand written agreement requiring payments twice a month. He kept his word and sent me money orders like clockwork. From the postmarks I could see where the Dead had been playing! The old band bus continued its long strange trip and, I'm sure, has even more tales to tell, if it could talk . . .

As I said, Things were good as we played our weekly gig at Feathers. Kermit, the last soundman I worked with, had a hefty Turbosound system that sounded amazing in that big room. The Phil Delta Band was now a six-piece outfit with Clinton playing pedal steel again, and George back on keyboards. I don't mean to sound biblical here, but as it was in the beginning, drinking was still a regular part of doing our kind of work and some of us handled it better than others. George unfortunately had a serious problem with alcohol, so playing in a bar was a kind of dangerous environment for him. Like many alcoholics, he learned to manage it well except for an occasional tumble off the wagon. Before one of our nights at Feathers, Clinton and Geroge went MIA. No one at the hotel had seen them. I finally found them both in Clinton's room, where they had pulled the mattress onto the floor and were both laying on it, laughing, and drunk as skunks. Apparently one thing had led to another, and . . . at least they were dressed! That was the beginning of the end for George's stint in the band, by his own choice.

Ron began having schedule conflicts and was backing off some of our dates. Luckily my former guitar man, Jim Ohlschmidt, had been playing bass in a Sheboygan-area Top 40 band and was available to fill-in for Ron on a few occasions. Having both Jim and Clinton at work onstage again brought back memories of the former band and all the crazy fun nights we played. Unfortunately things were becoming less and less like they used to be. As always, most folks loved us and our music, but line dancing was becoming a big deal. Don't get me wrong, folks on dance floors everywhere we played made the whole formula work - for the band, for the bar, and for the customers. Line dancing changed a couple of key elements in that formula. Line dancers wanted bands to perform an entire playlist of songs to fit their dancing style. To stay focused on their steps, they didn't drink a whole lot, and they started showing up in droves. It felt like the days of someone like Dancin' Dan getting out there and tearing up the floor freestyle were long gone.

The Phil Delta Band had several more personnel departures which pretty much disbanded (pun intended) the group as it had been. I carried on for a while with Scott May on keys and Paul Spitz on drums, along with a couple of FIB pickers Scott knew, but the sun was setting on my time as a country singer and band leader in Wisconsin and Illinois. The last band I worked with was a local blues outfit called the Shuffle Aires, featuring the amazing Al Ek, who is entertaining folks in Las Vegas these days. The band also included Milwaukee electric guitarist Jim Eanelli, a veteran of many different musical endeavors, including Colour Radio, Blem-Blem, and his own group Milk Train.

Jim recently reminded me of the time we played a juicy corporate event, which might have been in Marshfield, with like a noon start on a Sunday. This was after playing a typical late-night Saturday show in MIlwaukee, so we had to hustle, bleary-eyed, to make the three-hour drive and get there in time to set-up. I wasn't using a soundman anymore and was just dialing in the channels myself from onstage. I don't recall why, but the Shuffle Aires regular drummer, Bill Seibert, wasn't on this Sunday date, so Scooter agreed to fill in and play this nice little payday with me.

The event was at a race track with a grandstand on one side. A tent was set up for us on a raised platform, with horizontal metal bars about three feet high going around three sides, like fencing in a cattle lot, with the one side open. There were food tents and picnic tables on the infield, which we thought was behind us. The side of the stage without the bars going across, which we thought was the front, faced the grandstand. At the time it made sense to set-up facing the open side of the stage so people could come up into the seats and enjoy the show once we started playing. After everything was dialed-in and ready, we launched into our first tune when a woman from the event approached me to say the band is facing the wrong direction. She tells me we are set-up backward. We received zero direction on our arrival, and now all our set up work would have to be redone. Scooter was livid! All a guitar player has to do in this situation is pick up his amp, turn it around, move his mic, and boom, done. Drummers have to mostly take apart their kit, turn it all around, and then reassemble and readjust. It's a lot of damn work, all because whoever was in charge of this corporate clambake wasn't paying attention to which direction the FRONT of the danged stage was facing!

We opened for Asleep At The Wheel at Summerfest that year, along with a few other shows, but by then the writing was on the wall, so to speak. Like I've said in these pages, change is the one thing you can count on, including that day when you realize it's time to do something else for a while. One of the beauties of music is that it's always there for you to come back to, or not. It's always there to make you feel good when you don't, or to be like a wise old friend when you don't have a flesh-and-blood one handy. After you play all those great songs like I played for so long, the words take on particularly deep meanings, the lines become encoded in your being, and the wisdom therein a comfort as you keep traveling your path through life. The words and music of my musical heroes, many of whom are now departed, still guide me along, and have made the journey more worthwhile than I could have ever imagined.

Chapter 28
NEVER SAY NEVER

If you had asked me back in the 1980s if I would ever write a book, my answer would probably have been, "Are you crazy? Absolutely not!" But here I am, writing the last chapter of this book on New Year's Day. It's taken almost a year to finish, but it was easier to write than I thought and, for the most part, it was exciting. I found myself reaching for my phone in the middle of the night, opening the note app, and keying-in my thoughts before they drifted off. It's like songwriting. When a good melody or a lyric comes to you, it's best to write it down right away because it will usually be gone by the next morning, if not sooner.

Another big part of the process was looking at all the stuff I saved in cardboard boxes from back then. Old band schedules not only rekindled many memories of where and when we played, but they added up to almost 2,200 performances! We averaged about 200 dates a year, with 1983 and 1984 being the busiest, at 234 and 225 dates, respectively. Considering that the average gig lasted about four hours (not including travel time), that's around 9,000 hours of being onstage. Thank goodness I was younger and had lots of energy. It was what I call "performance energy" because there's something that takes over when you step on stage. The bright lights shine, the audience lets you know they are happy you are there, and before you know it, everybody is having a great time. There's nothing quite like it.

The Phil-osopher in me says that endings in life are really not always endings. Many are actually beginnings. I believe that great music and great songs - when played well with honesty and a little love - can live on in a meaningful way long after the performance. Kind of like that road that really does go on forever . . . To me, the common thread in life is LOVE. It holds each of us together and connects us with others. In my opinion, sharing what we love with others is an essential part of life, especially when it comes to music.

Love is the reason I learned to sing and play, and to share that music with others. It turned out to be the greatest gift that I know how to give. It also makes me feel worthy and meaningful, so I get a whole lot out of it, too. Someone taught me a longtime ago that it is impossible to help someone else without also helping yourself. When the show is over and when your life is over what you have given and shared with others is all that matters. It is all of "you" that is left. It is your final encore. The rest is just stuff.

In my case, I was fortunate to have exceptionally talented musicians making music with me. Way more than just band members, they were my friends and remain so to this day - Scott Thayer ("Scooter"), my favorite drummer in the world who hung in there the longest (or I should say "put up with me the longest"), Jim Ohlschmidt on acoustic and electric guitars, along with occasional Dobro and mandolin, Daniel More' on bass guitar, and Clinton Snell on pedal steel guitar (which he tuned by ear between songs while I was yappin' away). My band existed before they joined, and after, but these four guys defined our sound and made Phil Delta and The River Delta Band a top-notch act in Milwaukee, or anywhere.

As mentioned earlier in these pages, not much would have ever happened for us were it not for our amazing fans! There are so many faces lingering in memory that I can no longer put a name to, but I will give a few direct shout-outs here for some of the longtime audience members that I haven't mentioned yet, like the identical twins, Jim and Bob (I could never get their names right so I called them both "Jim Bob"), who regularly drove all the way from Chicago to our Milwaukee gigs. Another fan who became a great friend, and who says I inspired him to start playing music himself is Ed Goff. I absolutely must mention Scott Harcourt, the "#2 Phil Delta Band Fan" (out of respect for Jackie, Fan #1). When Scott married his beautiful wife Terri I played at their wedding, and he was even a roommate of mine for a while. There aren't words to express the gratitude that I have to all of you.

Music has always been in my life and my family. From my Mom humming me lullabies as she rocked me in her arms as a baby to singing acapella from the Church Of Christ pews, where musical accompaniment was not allowed, along with both of my parents singing with me as I sat between them. I remember my first positive compliments for singing came from adults seated near me in church.

Music is eternal from the dawn of man through the end of time. It has also been a constantly significant staple in my being for as long as I can remember. I am honored to have played a small part in music's wide path through most everyone's life. It is the tune or lyrics that you hear and just cannot get out of your head. It can enhance every aspect of your life and make you a more fulfilled and happier person. It can influence how you perceive and treat others. Lack of it can build barriers and its presence can tear down walls. It can move you to tears when mingled with touching spoken words in a movie or a play with its ability to break through the strongest "tear gates" to reach deep into your soul and break the barriers of the strongest of constitutions to quiver your lips and water your eyes. It can pick you up when you are down and bring you down when your temper runs high. Music is simply magical.

I no longer have a band, but am living a wonderful life down in Nashville, and I still love making music. It all began when I held that first guitar. That changed my life forever. I pick up my guitar and play almost every night, trying to learn a new lick or write a song. I even wrote a song about this recently called "Concert For One" that includes the lines "No gear to carry, no cords to wrap-up, or other chores . . . And I always get an encore." Looking back on the trials and tribulations of this very meaningful portion of my life, I can't help but ask myself the question "Was the gettin' worth the go?" It surely was! Man, what a ride, and a heartful of wonderful memories. I sure hope you enjoyed reading this book, as much as I have enjoyed writing it. I'll leave you with the words of the late, great Jerry Jeff Walker who once said, "Life goes by so fast, but it's the way that you remember it that counts. So, tell it in a good way, even if you have to embellish it a little bit."

ACA Talent Agency promo shot

*First band promo flier with
Pabst Blue Ribbon Beer sponsorship*

*First River Delta Band members
with Mark Terek and Michael White*

Marlboro contest Band with Scott May and Joe Gorman

Memphis Music Heritage Festival band shot

Jim and Phil playing at Milwaukee Zoo

Phil with the Outlaw Women

Phil Delta on stage at Summerfest

Possibly the worst pic of Phil ever taken outside Myrtle hotel room after a long night

Bus on tracks getting to Painless' first wedding reception

*Phil after playing his first Summerfest gig
on the shores of Lake Michigan*